Stacking Stones

An Anthology of Short Tanka Sequences

M. Kei, Editor

Keibooks, Perryville, Maryland, USA, 2018

Keibooks
P O Box 346
Perryville, MD 21903
Keibooks@gmail.com

Table of Contents

Introduction:
Stone Into Light

Like stones stacked one on another by a meditative mind, tanka build into sequences. Each tanka, like a stone, is a unique and special piece in its own right, but when they are thoughtfully assembled with care for balance and beauty, they become something new. Each retains its individual character, but the gestalt says something more than each individually. The proximity of another tanka brings out the shape and color of the complementary pieces. Some contrast and some blend, but all fit together in a harmonious whole.

It is no surprise that ever since the invention of tanka, they have been strung together into longer sequences. The shortest possible is a pair of tanka, often given between friends or lovers, and many of those appear here. Others build gradually. Three, four, five, six, seven, or more tanka. In our anthology, they top out at thirteen. Previous experience has shown that sequences beyond thirteen are less common and require new techniques to manage the ever increasing numbers.

In addition, tanka sequences often occur in combination with other forms of poetry, commonly haiku, as well as prose. The latter is called 'tanka prose,' and has already published an anthology (*The Tanka Prose Anthology*, MET Press, 2008), but they are included here because tanka is a multivalent form of poetry that naturally pairs well with many variations, and we want to show short tanka sequences in all their possibilities.

More than a hundred poets and teams of poets from fourteen countries submitted over eleven hundred verses in more than two hundred sequences. While most were conventionally formatted, usually left-justified, occasional submissions, such as a five verse tanka mandala, required special handling. Collaborative compositions were especially complex with varying numbers of contributors.

Groups of contributors each came up with their own method for distinguishing the members' contributions.

Others chose to present a joint authorship in which no differentiation was made because they wanted the reader to experience the work as a seamless whole rather than as individual voices. I accepted whatever schemata the authors had chosen, but this required an upgrade to my record-keeping which had me pulling my hair while I adapted to the demands of diverse collaborations. The patience of contributors when I made corrections is appreciated.

The complexity and the quality of the submissions made this the most difficult anthology I've edited, but also one of the most rewarding. The pieces chosen for the anthology showcase a wide variety of subject matter and approaches. Out of the eighty-seven pieces accepted for publication, sixteen contain prose as well as tanka, eighteen are collaborative works by two or more authors, one is a tanka prose with found tanka, and one is a mandala of five verses. Here and there are inclusions of kyoka, ryuka, sedoka, and haiku.

Shaped tanka, in which tanka are formatted to create a non-linear presentation on the page are rare, so I was pleased to get one. I have previously seen circular tanka and crossed-shaped tanka sequences, but not many others. Matthew Caretti's 'Moab Mandala' can be read as multiple intersecting sequences. For example, the left top tanka, middle tanka, and left lower tanka can be read as a sequence of three. The same for the right side, as well as the top, bottom, and diagonals. Likewise, each pair can be read together, or opposite corners, or any other configuration. This creates a kaleidoscope of small sequences, each of which works, and each of which complements the others. This is a masterful use of tanka's fungibility to arrange and rearrange discrete elements into meaningful new relationships. It's also a headache for the editor; the mandala form does not readily transpose to book format. I opted for an oversized page, but even so, it still feels cramped. Tanka mandalas would do best in a large format with plenty of white space.

Another unique and masterful non-standard piece is Bruce England's 'Lover for a Day,' in which individual reviewers for the French movie *Lover for a Day* accidentally committed poetry while writing reviews. It was England's good luck to stumble on them, and it bespeaks his attentive eye that he recognized the poetry inherent in the quotidian stuff of reviews by the general public. Found tanka, like other forms of found poetry, take words from some other source and arrange them as poetry. The resulting work is a fair use under the copyright law of the United States. Proper credit is given to each contributor.

The anthology is divided into ten sections thematically. Each sequence contributes to the larger sequence of the chapter. Each chapter contributes to the larger sequence of the whole. Thus it is not only an anthology of sequences, but a sequence of sequences. Links and shifts, variations in length and authorship, and changes in approach sustain interest throughout the full length. An anthology is not simply a collection of unrelated items; the contents must work together to create a greater whole.

This is particularly true of 'Red Lace' where romantic relationships are tinged with sadness, then frustration, infidelity, and violence. By the end of the chapter, when Martin McKellar and Barry Simms find age undermining not only their manhood but their sense of self, resonances with the earlier works fill the reader with conflicting emotions. Certainly when we read 'Sequence #4' straight, it is a poignant tale of old men slipping into senescence, but the suspicions engendered by those earlier works taint our sympathy. Especially coming hard on the heels of the #MeToo movement. While it is tempting to hope for each of us to reach a restful old age, the truth is, all of us must also be held to account for the actions of our lives. Old age does not absolve us.

These shifting meanings due to contiguity are what we call 'multivalency' in tanka, or controlled ambiguity. This flexibility of meaning is one of tanka's great strengths. The poet's control of ambiguity means that while the tanka itself is perfectly clear, it carries with it connotations and suggestions that raise compatible interpretations. Tanka are like stones thrown into a still pond: each pebble creates its own rings of meaning, but they intersect with those of other pebbles. When tanka coexist with other groups of tanka, new and complex resonances are discovered. Not all of these are intended by the author, but it doesn't matter. The reader is a co-creator. The passive reader who expects the author to explain it to him will be frustrated; tanka do not open to those who do not open to tanka. Tanka are stepping stones, not highways. In other words, the goal is not to reach the end, but to enjoy the journey.

When tanka are organized in groups, they usually form either strings or sequences. The simplest explanation is that strings are loose groupings while sequences have some kind of structure. In short sequences, the difference between string and structure blurs. Sticking to shorter sequences was a deliberate editorial choice: longer groups of tanka need some kind of organizing principle to organize the reader's attention. They function very differently than shorter sequences because of this.

What then, are the organizing principles of short tanka sequences? The simplest, and perhaps oldest, form of structure is the call and response. One poet writes a tanka, and the other responds to it. This type of structure has gained the name of 'responsive tanka.' We see this with many pairs of poets: Michael H. Lester and Joy McCall, Akane and Dave Read, Taura Scott and dalton perry, Jan

Foster and Anne Benjamin to name just a few appearing in this anthology.

In 'Weather Report,' Jan Foster and Anne Benjamin are discussing the same subject, but they do not repeat each other. Each tanka evolves the sequence, leading step by meteorological step to the denouement. The consistent use of a theme (weather) with varying details maintains the reader's interest and builds suspense. We rarely see two writers who work so well together in sharing a theme while avoiding redundancy. Each poet contributes new imagery consistent with the previous verses that expands instead of repeating the emotional content. Any tanka picked out at random reads well on its own; they are autonomous.

This is the way responsive sequences ought to be written; too often one poet winds up merely echoing what the other has said. Redundant tanka weaken a sequence by sapping its vitality. Every tanka in a group must have a good reason for being there. Because responsive sequences are often composed in conversation, poets neglect to edit them. They have forgotten that what began as conversation must now be edited into literature. Items of great interest to the participants will bore the reader unless the literary quality and organization make them interesting.

When there are least three poets in the group, a different kind of structure can develop, as with the Banyan Poets who contributed 'Stepping Into the Light.' With each poet limited to one poem, repetition is inherently difficult. Instead, each tanka provokes a shift. This, in turn, poses a challenge to artistic control. When there are only two poets in a sequence, they generally have a shared understanding of what they are doing, but the greater the number of poets participating, the more difficult that is to achieve. Multi-author sequences run the risk of wandering randomly.

The example by the Banyan Poets shows how to balance autonomy and control so that the parts create a coherent whole. The opening verse by Leslie Bamford features trees and a birth mother, but the second tanka, by Robyn Cairns, shifts those ideas to flowers and a father to express a different kind of maternal relationship. The third verse, by Marianne Paul, picks up the theme that things are not always as they seem, while the fourth verse, by Samar Ghose, reminds us that we shouldn't worry too much about what others think. The author of the final verse has a special responsibility. They must be complete the sequence in a way that satisfies and finalizes all that has come before. Barbara Hays accomplishes this skillfully. Her final two lines, "I'm riding this tide all the way," summarizes the overarching theme that emerged from the distinct contributions of eight poets.

'Link and shift' is a classic technique of tanka sequences dating back to medieval Japan when renga was a popular literary form. Today it is better known through haiku where sequences have been popular for decades. In spite of the haiku association, link and shift was a fundamental technique developed to manage lengthy tanka sequences dating back to the medieval period in Japan. Old tanka sequences were commonly created in one hundred and one thousand poem lengths. In one case, the pirates of the Murakami Suigun created a sequence of more than thirty thousand tanka over a three hundred year period. (See ATPO 27 for more information and samples of their work.)

Some Western critics claim that the urge to create sequences is evidence of tanka's deficiency; they see it as too small to address 'serious' topics. Regular readers of tanka disagree. They know that everything from the atomic bomb to protest marches have been addressed in tanka. The creation of sequences has been inherent in tanka from the beginning. Tanka are like stones that can be used to build anything from walls to gardens, the parts mortared together via prose or other inclusions.

Tish Davis shows us how this can work. In 'While Running the Course,' she intercuts snippets of a Navajo song with her tanka. Ostensibly about a woman running a race, it is actually about the much larger topic of growing old with grace and finding our place in the universe. Mundane details such as a dying iPod are interspersed with moments of community as when a church volunteer passes out water bottles. That, in turn, lets her link to the eagle soaring overhead, and to come to the conclusion—even as she passes over the relics of American industrialization— that the world "is lovely indeed."

Although tanka lends itself well to minimalism as in Davis' piece, brevity is not the definition of tanka. Any number of sequences and tanka prose pieces illustrate how sometimes more is more, whether it is Amelia Fielden or Richard Grahn with their elegies, or Gerry Jacobson or Christopher Shawn Rathburn who dwell at length about the bodily indignities of being human.

At fifteen tanka, Rathburn's 'Crucible' is actually longer than the limit of thirteen in the guidelines, but it presents a different mode of writing tanka than is commonly seen. It is what the Japanese of the earliest centuries called, "direct expression." Instead of using images and symbols to make his point, he comes right out and says it. Further, he writes in a strict 5-7-5-7-7 pattern of syllables which has generally been abandoned in English because it usually creates verses that are too dense and heavy. Tanka are supposed to be ballet dancers, not linebackers.

Rathburn's approach is typical of someone who is new to tanka, but at the same time, unlike most newcomers, he has managed to sustain his concept by writing naturally. His lines are neither enjambed nor padded; he has matched his form and content to one another with sufficient skill that it seems artless, naive even. Speaking as an editor who has seen over a hundred thousand tanka, trust me when I say it's rare to find a poet that can make 5-7-5-7-7 work in English. Rathburn takes us to the limit of what can be considered 'short' for a tanka sequence.

Topics in the anthology range from the humorous to the sublime. Some of the carnal renderings are Michael H. Lester's 'What Smells?' regarding a miner of the gold rush acquiring the company of a transgender lover for the evening, and the equally physical, but more elevated approach of R.K. Singh whose paramour wears red lace in 'Love's Spirit.' Pravat Kumar Padhy finds the muse in science, not art, and likens his lover's scarred face to the moon with its craters. Although the pulse of life throbs for everyone, it inevitably leads to loss. Everyone leaves, whether it's baby bats dying in Lorne Henry's 'Heatwave,' or Dave Read's 'Boys' who are no longer interested in spending time with their father (unless they need him to drive). Personal losses of many sorts are frequent in tanka literature and are amply addressed in this anthology.

Everyone leaves. Sometimes literally, as in Richard St. Clair who leaves North Dakota as far in his past as he can, or Elizabeth Howard who comes to understand why the old place was named, 'Bitter Spring.' Matthew Caretti, Lorne Henry, and Joy McCall all try to go home in 'Homestead,' 'Cast Out,' and 'ruined,' respectively, but they discover you can never go home. We are all afflicted with boulders we can't move, as Susan Burch shares in the opening tanka of the collaborative 'Becoming.' Yet there is still a measure of grace available to us as her six writing partners show us. Moving beyond, Malintha Perera soothes our mind with 'Zazenkai,' while Debbie Strange and ai li are guided by their dreams in 'spectral' and 'dream tanka.' Yet it is Patricia Prime and Giselle Maya who lead us to the divine in their 'Sacred Sites.'

Ultimately, there is a 'time to quit' (Larry Kimmel and Joy McCall), when the 'Bitter Stacks' (Sanford Goldstein) of the world become too heavy to bear. Yet if we stick it out, we discover that 'Keeping Our Promise' (Leslie Bamford) gives a new lease on life. The key to redemption is found in 'Wild Swan,' by A. A. Marcoff. A luminously beautiful piece of tanka prose, it offers some of the some of the most masterful run-on sentences in the English language (each perfectly punctuated):

> and the sudden metamorphosis of the moment, the urge to shape life and go, to be reborn, to emerge from the womb of these chambers, in the loosening of time, the coming of fresh green meditations, a surge of green shoots in my thoughts, a latent pink blossom from bud and branch, blossom that flows now with petal and a bloom rooted in a sudden new world . . .

In the end, it is the swans that lift us. Though we are drowned, the luminescence of their wings rises up, carrying us with it, to an "amazement of light," as Debbie Strange puts it. We have come a long way on our journey, from home and hardship, past fear and friendship, through love and loss and the bitter disappointment that we are not the people we thought we would be. And yet, there at the very end, when we stop chasing after whatever it is our hearts long to catch, peace will come to us and lay a numinous spell upon our hearts.

M. Kei
Editor, *Stacking Stones*
17 July 2018

One:
Much Like a
Polaroid

Living Room Gallery

How mom might find herself on our wall, posing with fruit, or skimpy in her early days, or later amidst pole shadows, but most of all I think she would choose the overlapping horizons, sea bells, bright blooming hills, distant city of lights, sunset dwindling all framed with fragile fringes where past meets past in limitless blue.

hokusai's great wave
the sound of it rising
over her head
she relaxed into the swell
in the vanishing

Kath Abela Wilson, Pasadena and Santa Barbara, California, USA

Work Desk

no difference now
than when I was twenty —
put on the coffee,
sit by a quiet window
and write things down

kick-starting
this mule mind:
the elixir of coffee,
as morning pulls the sun
up by its rusty chain

my desk today —
a shamble
of papers, drafts, bills,
the debris field
of wasted days

no one pays
too much attention,
poet — be prepared
to labor in dim light
for the love of it

so many billion words
poured into
old notebooks—
it does nothing;
time has its way with us

one gets older,
one turns into text:
look at me, spattered
with words, most of which
can no longer be made out

at 2 o'clock
Barking Dog next door
finally gives up;
for another hour
I'll work on my poem

Roger Jones, Texas, USA

Spun

spinning flowers
a deep yellow —
another cup
of hibiscus flavored tea
and this small-talk

> *the artist*
> *brushes her cheek*
> *passionflower*
> *what color is it*
> *in the dark*

on my day off
at a downtown exhibit
staring intently
at the reds
in a Gaugin painting

> *deep green*
> *blood of the earth*
> *blurs*
> *the edges of the path*
> *in a self-portrait landscape*

Matsukaze, Texas, USA
Kath Abela Wilson, California, USA

Mapplethorpe

long-haired people
of the seventies
in black and white[1]
with sunglasses
and bunches of flowers

his muse
stares into her past
their future
does her long dark hair
need cutting[2]

selfie . . .
his face pressed
against the wall
is he hiding
from his own camera[3]

side by side . . .
a leg points upwards
toes extended[4] . . .
a bum fills another frame
bare, black, life size[5]

she stares at me
critically
out of time
I hear my name called
by a Jewish mother[6]

about to die
the artist salutes us
with a skull-topped cane
his eyes follow me
as I leave the gallery[7]

Gerry Jacobson, New York City, New York, USA

[1]*'Robert Mapplethorpe — the perfect medium'. Art Gallery of New South Wales, 2018*

[2]*Patti Smith, c1974, gelatin silver photograph.*

[3]*Untitled (self-portrait) c1974, gelatin silver photograph.*

[4]*Lisa Lyon, 1981, printed 2016, gelatin silver photograph.*

[5]*Ron Simms, 1980, gelatin silver photograph.*

[6]*Louise Nevelson, 1986, printed 1990, gelatin silver photograph.*

[7]*Self-portrait, 1988, platinum photograph.*

Lover for a Day (2017):

Found Tanka and Sedoka Film Reviews in Rottentomatoes.com

Synopsis: After a severe breakup, the only place 23-year-old Jeanne has to stay in Paris is the small flat belonging to her father, Gilles. But when Jeanne arrives, she finds her father living with a new girlfriend her own age, Arianne. Both young women are looking for love in a city filled with possibilities. — Rotten Tomatoes.

Philippe Garrel, Director, b/w, 76 minutes, aka *L'amant d'un jour.* Eric Caravaca (Gilles), Esther Garrel (Jeanne), Louise Chevillotte (Ariane)

Your heart isn't
likely to soar during
this poetic drama
but it might ache
with recognition

Jamie Dunn

This is cinema
of feelings, of passions,
of men and women
who love each other, although
not always in unison

Javier Porta Fouz

Characters are fixed
they have no arc and Garrel
seems to prefer them
learning nothing
from their experiences

April Wolfe

The pleasure of
Lover for a Day lies in
watching lives
being lived: bare, open,
aggrieved and unjudged

Simon Crook

Oh hell,
it's refreshing to see
a woman
give a man a taste
of his own Don Juan

Erica Abeel

Garrel
offers a film
much like a Polaroid
joyfully impure and
with fuzzy outlines

Juanma Ruiz

Storytelling style
is like a great pop ballad,
lyrics to the point without
digressions, yet still
containing a wealth of feelings
through the most economic means

Carson Lund

Garrel's detractors
contend that he always
makes the same film
his defenders say
that's the point

Ben Croll

Monochrome stylings
and a plot laced with ennui,
it might be the most
French film ever made, but
there's no denying Garrel's craft

Simon Kinnear

An alluring and
very elegantly crafted
though largely predictable
romantic dramedy
it should do well where this French
auteur is known and esteemed

Pamela Pianezza

Curated by Bruce England, California, USA

The Bard Coined It

I say good morning across
an empty bed
Death lies on her
like an untimely frost
trapped in diary, her bookmark

Romeo and Juliet

I empty my father's ashes
in running water
He that dies pays all debts
moon fragments
dissolve in the river

The Tempest

after the screams
chilling silence
dark alleyway
The Devil incarnate
within

Henry V

winter chill
as cold as any stone
the homeless
fails to survive
the night

Henry V

in white embroidery
on the windowpane
blizzard-prints
as pure
as the driven snow

The Winter's Tale

Flower Moon
dash'd all to pieces
summer wind
I disintegrate
in the lake waters

The Tempest

setting sun
bathes skyscrapers in gilded hue
all that glitters is not gold
under the wig
her thinning hairline

Merchant of Venice

my shadow
sneaks out
in the dark
brevity is the soul of wit
the Gettysburg Address

Hamlet

share them
reinterpret them
to your *heart's content*
just remember
the Bard coined it

Vijay Joshi, New Jersey, USA

Two:
The Starless Night

Turning

winter-worn
the trees shed themselves
of old burdens
as the year turns
on a spinning wheel

colour returns
in fragmented bursts
a snowdrop-filled bank
the crocus beds
shining lights

wakefulness unwinds
to longer days
clipped evenings
the cull of summer
burns beneath you

Joanna Ashwell, Northeast England

Butterfly Song

a butterfly
clings to a blossom . . .
its wings
flutter in the notes
of peach fragrance

the butterfly
catches golden rays
on a sunflower—
Mum hangs her silk scarf
to drive off a crow

a butterfly
flies forward . . .
oh, please don't be in haste,
there may be
a thorny rose

a butterfly
beats its wings
in autumn sun
the old woman
waves a red maple leaf

a butterfly
in winter rain . . .
the ice on my hair
thickening
on its wings

a butterfly
perched on a temple bell . . .
the chimes
of its vibration
reach the Old Monk's ears

David He, Zhuanglang, China

Stepping Into the Light

green boughs above
the pine needles
in this forest
every tree is
my birth mother   LB

our bare feet
in nasturtiums—
since dad's death
I get to know my mum
as Judy   RC

the long-stem leaf
scuttling by my boot
is really a mouse
the brain sees the truth
it wants   MP

dance
even if you can't
they say
in the wilderness of your heart
the leaf litter is airborne   SG

therapy session;
sitting by the window
I watch
the dandelion seeds
dislodge in the breeze   JM

déjà vu caresses
my arm
in the empty
hotel room
perfume lingers   CW

striding toward me
unknown
but familiar
I paint her house
she paints my life   RB

salt breezes—
the happy sound
of gulls
I'm riding this tide
all the way   BH

Banyan Tree Poets, Australia, Canada, United States of America

Leslie Bamford, Canada (LB)
Robert Bamford, Canada (RB)
Robyn Cairns, Australia (RC)
Samar Ghose, Australia (SG)
Barbara Hay, USA (BH)
Jayashree Maniyil, Australia (JM)
Marianne Paul, Canada (MP)
Christine White, Canada (CW)

The Spinning Wheel

milkweed blooms
at the meadow's edge
she waits
for the monarch's blessing
under a shattered sky

one strand snaps
and the tapestry ravels —
at dusk
a mockingbird sings
the old crone's song

soft rain falling
through a starless night
she weaves
its many-colored threads
into a shroud for the earth

Jenny Ward Angyal, North Carolina, USA

Turn, Turn

In a world torn by war and corruption, I fret about the things I throw away, the things I lose, the things that go and never return.

first day of summer,
spitting watermelon seeds
into the compost heap,
a few months later,
I have more watermelons

M. Kei, Chesapeake Bay, USA

Sent Yesterday

burning sage
with a joyful heart   m
in the wind
newly burned holes
of a reed flute   k

purchased fresh honey—
untied shoes   m
in the way
during tai chi
the sound of texts buzzing   k

purchasing
black calla lilies   m
midmorning rain
after midnight
the scent of kumquats   k

watching 'Versailles'
a cluster of grapes   m
omniscient eyes
in Paris the carousel
sings like my mother   k

twilight sky
color of a red cockscomb—   m
more sugar in my tea
a white peony
the taste of sesame   k

eating fried eggs
with my father   m
loneliness the color grey
slicing mozzarella into hearts
for her last meal   k

girl with insect eyes
—long train ride   m
north
to yellow mountain
the time of cicadas   k

red peppers
fluttering
you play koto   m
wind in my hair
and fresh lemon basil   k

Matsukaze, Texas, USA
Kath Abela Wilson California, USA

so much still unknown

always compliant
to the *leave no trace*
ethics
we stack memories
in our hearts

> *retirement day*
> *I choose to forget*
> *the wasted years*

wishing on a stone
to return
again and again
to place a stone
on our cairn

> *with a toothbrush*
> *and cleaning solution*
> *I remove*
> *the lichens of age*
> *from our parents' headstone*

a clamour of rooks
guarding the entrance
to Stonehenge
so much still unknown
about our past

passing
the small ochre mine
by canoe
I wonder if an ancestor
will say hello

moonless sky
hiking from a cairn
to the next

ready to take
my place
in the night sky
a final dance
with the aurora

Luminita Suse, Canada
Mike Montreuil, Canada

Three:
Red Lace

Love's Spirit

Love's spirit descends
and melds into her body
lending it new life:
I'm amazed how the unknown
becomes one with her beauty

a happier image
with salubrious top
turns rapturous
as she tamps her love
with watery lipstick

it's not ageing
but eternal delight:
she under me
smooth belly, nude necking
slow stroking parting flesh

shaped like a bird
a drop of water lands
on her breast:
my breath jumps to kiss it
before her pelvic flick

the beads of sweat
on her breasts do not touch
her years or face
in candlelight her shadow
is more restrained than my thought

she stoops low
to the bottom shelf
in black jeans
her curves flattering and
red lace groping her hips

she undresses in
dim light perfumes her body
fills the room with herself:
we hit the hay together
drowning in each other

raising
her hard drink
heavenward:
to my man, lover of
animals, soft in sex

R. K. Singh, India

Wartime Love

I kept his letters
some written from the front line
some from hospital
words of love outweighed the woe
though sometimes tears left their smudge

weeks would go by without news
then three or four come at once

now he returns home
in a wheelchair, thin and pale
I see past the scars
to the man I used to know
the man he still is inside

he showers me with kisses
four years of pent-up passion

Tracy Davidson, Warwickshire, England

May-December

a girl I loved
that spring—
honeysuckle in the air
the hour she came,
the hour she left

spring rain—
her father drives through the woods
honking, searching for us;
we step out of the wet trees,
laughing

down cracked streets
I bike home
or swing back by her house,
past her window, where roses
patiently climb a trellis

bright galleon clouds
passing over
with the September wind—
we have the whole field
to ourselves, to watch

someone's online photos
of our old summer camp—
the footbridge I took
summer nights to her cabin,
all its handrails gone now

I sit scribbling
poems to my beloved,
the canary behind me
scattering seed
all over its cage

Market Street corner
in holiday fog
under champagne streetlights—
enjoying the buzz
of our new union

Roger Jones, Texas, USA

just enough touch

another disagreement . . .
he goes to the bar
I go to the bath
and decorate myself
in flowers

floating in stock,
quince and violas
I stop analyzing
what's for me
and what's not

a mandala
of blossoms
on my womb
trusting what life is
meant to be

stacking pennies,
dimes and nickels
all that's left
of his
dark night

a tiny pebble
in the ruffled sheets
just enough touch
to make
me cry

Jessica Malone Latham, California, USA

Bar Girl

when I'm tired
of noise and clamour
I slip away from the bar
and hide up awhile
with the back room guy

    where does she go
    the shy girl at the bar
    who slips away
    reappears with a broad grin
    an untucked blouse and tousled hair?

Joy McCall, Norwich, England
Michael H. Lester, Los Angeles, California, USA

café express

he was with her now
across the café
his ring
jangling in her purse
with those unreturned calls

> *the burden*
> *of being a man*
> *conflicted by desire*
> *and the inability*
> *to ask directions*

always the lady
in waiting
with her croissant
and espresso
what a flake

> *taking the tip*
> *from off of a table*
> *he bought a map*
> *to show the cabby*
> *maybe she's here*

she searched
from café to café
nothing left for her
but a broken heel
and chapped lips

his french
so poor
even
their kisses
failed to translate

was it the strength
of the espresso
that held her
or his grasp
on her heart

the note read
come home sober
with coffee and flowers
we need to talk
about this ring

Taura Scott, California, United States
dalton perry, California, United States

What if

what if I'd turned
Jane's head a little more
before she decided
what she thought
she ought to think

what if I'd closed
the filing room door,
dimmed the light
would I have been sure
what Louise followed me inside for

when Patricia held
the end of my measuring tape
what if I'd wound it in
that extra bit until no distance
was left between our lips

what if Diane had insisted
I held my arms
more tightly about her,
drawn her closer,
would any harm have come of it

what if during
Kate's alcoholic stupor
I'd taken advantage
would she have even remembered
what we did

Geoffrey Winch, England

three unwise tanka

through the paper-thin
partition wall
the sound of her father ejaculating
in the maid's room
hear no evil

the kittens writhing
in a gunny sack
bound for
the bayou
see no evil

her poison pen gossip
a collage of overheard
motel liaisons
and village incest
speak no evil

ai li, london, england, and singapore

Reflections on Going Out

no-one but you ever sees
your bathroom mirror's
mist
slowly revealing
your dreary flesh

friends never witness
you standing before
your cheval glass
disguising the person
you really are

only your reflection
in your dressing-table mirror
scrutinises
the way
you brush your hair

only you catch yourself
winking and silly-grinning
in your hallway mirror
moments before
you go out the door

friends recognise you
by your gait and stride
and they greet you
as the friend
they believe you to be

Geoffrey Winch, England

Sequence #4

solemn bells
tone the time of day
the grey sky
smiles with a glint
of the sun

I worry the tree
Is outgrowing its look of
Hand-trimmed perfection.
Then there is the old mirror
That says the same about me.

startled
by the old man
in the bathroom with me
is that really
my reflection?

The summer garden,
Its many green feathers held
In a spider's web,
A fluttering reflection
Of my unfocused mind.

the fluttering reflection
of sunlight
on my cell phone screen
pulls my attention
unfocuses my mind

In a tiny room
With walls of summer rain,
There are no windows.
Am I growing more separate
From the world, or less?

> *rain stained wall*
> *remnants*
> *of a leaky window*
> *the beautiful stain*
> *decreases my property value*

Martin McKellar, Gainesville, Florida, USA
Billy Simms, Hamilton, Ohio, USA

Four:
Out of the Doorway

What's That Smell?

mud-caked boots
a rifle over her shoulder
beady eyes
she hasn't shaved in days
smells like a mule's ass

the gold rush
brings all kinds to the river
men like me
I've been panning for months
found no big nuggets yet

I start a fire
to cook up some venison
she brings beans
a fifth of some cheap whiskey
a bushel full of tall tales

when night falls
she sashays into my tent
dims the kerosene lamp
it gets down in the 30s
even grizzled cowpokes get cold

come morning
she's already up and gone
all that's left
an empty whiskey bottle
the smell of a mule's ass

Michael H. Lester, Sutter's Mill, Coloma, California, USA

Muse of Science

scars
on her face
I console
how the craters glorify
the whiteness of the moon

sitting alone
in deepmidnight
I harvest
wisdom of consciousness
the part of the enlightened galaxy

in exchange
for my welcome-smile
the aliens
bridge our blue earth
with another milky path

the rising urge
of wave after wave . . .
the moon
whispers gentle swell
of the passionate desire

I return
from the crematorium
with moist eyes
at the entrance gate
a robot with a stony face

the river sways
the bagful of wilted leaves . . .
in a wooden boat
recalling Archimedes' principle
the crowded pilgrims try to readjust

cosmic call
for the earth scientists . . .
space ladder bridging
conference in Mars town
with the interstellar beings

my daughter quizzes
about the wall painting
I revisit
school physics of the falling apple
over Newton sitting under the tree

a radiant street
deep in the space
the Milky Way
leads to the glittering art
of the big-bang ballet

the girl reaches
the far-off distant planet
the aliens delivered
a parcel of gene box draped
with ribbons of Dolly sheep

Pravat Kumar Padhy, India

Crossings

biting into a vermilion apple
with night coming
light traffic
and silence

> *the lights go out*
> *at the drive-thru window*
> *a crow*
> *pecks an apple*
> *before becoming night*

just waking up
a moment gathering myself
stretching and
wringing shadows out of my bones

> *the triumph of youth!*
> *this afternoon sun —*
> *that time*
> *in my life*
> *I conquered my shadow*

on this summer day
an old woman stops in the middle
of the pedestrian crossings
searching for a memory

> *the warm breath*
> *of a summer breeze —*
> *we listen*
> *as Grandma tells*
> *stories of her youth*

Akane, Texas, USA
Dave Read, Calgary, Alberta, Canada

the wind through the web

the cleaner's broom
sweeps away the web
and the spider
one husk and a single leaf
in memory of lost love

is it the pain
or the sad story
that brings tears?
all this going and coming
even wind, through the web, gone

a spider
in the dustballs
under the bed
snuggled up and so cozy
the kitten, one eye open

Joy McCall, Norwich, England
Don Wentworth, Pennsylvania, USA

Tilt

this early shift,
the sun starts
its rise —
my seasonal depression
tilts with the earth

dark
when leaving; dark
coming home —
my house is a castle
of hundred watt bulbs

the moon and stars
behind the clouds tonight —
we gaze
at old sitcoms
whose actors are dead

unable to leave
for a winter
getaway —
I curse my children
for going to school

another day
without any sun —
passing
the bottle
of vitamin D

Dave Read, Alberta, Canada

Dark Lady

right hip's dodgy . . .
oh *gluteus medeus*
please hold me up
and let me walk
a little longer

my body's
fighting inflammation
caffeine
is my drug of choice
today's a four-cup day

naked
and vulnerable
I don
the hospital gown
ready for the sword to fall

I surrender
into nothingness
emerge
into consciousness . . .
how time has flown

it's a long night
in a hospital bed
on my back
dawn is grey and groggy
a grim nurse brings some pills

who lays down
the sacred laws of hip replacement
don't cross your legs
don't twist or bend
keep your bum above your knees

floating along
with panadeine forte
always asking
'who am I?'
I begin to wonder

reclining
in the arms
of the night nurse . . .
dark lady please give me
a clexane injection

oh that
my bowels could move
so that
I would be discharged
from this damn hospital

my case mother
décolleté
questions me
about ageing
and disability

cared for
fed and nurtured
and yet those doubts . . .
shouldn't I be the one
doing the caring?

oh Yarralumla
cooled by lakeside breeze
your pavements
are crumbling
and I am on crutches

up and down
a concrete ramp
with crutches
I close my eyes
once more on a hillside

Gerry Jacobson, Canberra, ACT, Australia

History Is Made of Broken Crockery

    The Dutch have been dredging a canal. All the items they found in it, all the bits of broken detritus of the centuries, they have photographed and put online. I am absorbed. I have to look at every broken piece of crockery and every lost key stretching back a thousand years.

    Many of the items are expected: buttons, boathooks, and bottles. Worn out shoes. Others are not. Why so many spurs at the bottom of a canal?

    toy soldiers
    found in the dredge spoil,
    tossed
    into the canal by
    children weary of war

    M. Kei, Chesapeake Bay, USA

Dreamories

In the early hours of a brand new day, I back my car out of the garage and park it temporarily on the street. The ominous sky above tangles in my mind with the distant memories of a long-lost wife. Slowly my thoughts turn and wander around the corner where I find myself wondering if animals have dreams . . .

> Thunder brings the rain—
> my cat curls up
> to take a nap
> on the dry side
> of the window.

What I've discovered is that dreams are bittersweet and memories are just along for the ride. Driving down the back alleys of my mind I see a sign that reads "NO U-TURN." Breaking that law is just not possible. We're not programmed that way . . .

> Rays bleeding
> through wounded skies . . .
> across the lake
> a skipping stone eventually
> complies with gravity.

A car door opens somewhere inside my thoughts. I step out and begin to wonder where I'll be tomorrow. I wonder if the squirrels in the almond trees believe in God. I wonder if God believes in me. I'm wandering through a forest of moments, dancing with my waking memories but the waking's really all I need to begin another dream . . .

In the taste of morning
a fleeting dance
unfurls
as sunlight
greets the leaves.

Richard Grahn, in the Hypnopompic State of Illinois, USA

Elegies : Some Tanka Reflections

my slow days
in gas-fired warmth
looking out
at grey winds sweeping
the remnants of autumn

finally
on the elm young leaves
fluttering
the morning after
my friend's last breath

spring sunlight
on four dear faces
by a cherry tree
frothed with pink flowers —
all gone now, every one

Gran and Pop
waltzing, harmonizing
'Always'
in those days of roses
with sweet-scented hearts

all that remains
on a windless blue day
his ashes
settle into the hole
under our eucalypt

the driftwood
we left on the beach
the dreams
we dared to confide . . .
to whom do they belong now

engagement photo
at Lake Yamanaka
the mountain
rises snow-streaked behind,
in the foreground just us

my mother said
"this one's a keeper" —
she was wrong
he drifted away
into an early death

shifting
from foot to foot
edging
out of the doorway
my stepson leaves home

bare limbs
now clad in green leaves —
I glance away
and the children move on
into their distant lives

Amelia Fielden, Australia

blue danube

another way
of dying
filling up
your room
with soul memories

an old
gilt hairbrush
coty loose powder
dusting
a lost generation

the chandelier
now dark
waltzes from
the danube
echo

your jewel box
pins and coronets
tiaras and cameos
basking on
fading red velvet

ai li, london, england, and singapore

Five:
Everyone Leaves

Compass

steer me there
within a dream
the land of honey
where hope runs
into every valley

show me the way
across craggy beaches
where the tide rages
with no port to land
for the flying sail

compass point
pinned to my heart
stir yourself
find me a nook
to settle inside

Joanna Ashwell, Northeast England

Off Highway 1, North of Santa Cruz

On the trail down
we carry wine and food
and other gear
the bonfire is alive
we stand as close as we can

The last of the sun
pink above the horizon
music is playing
some couples are dancing
kids play beyond the light

You pull me down
our jackets open, our hands
slide under more clothes
we think about sleeping here
but the tide is high tonight

The fire is shrinking
the night starts to feel ancient
fog is stepping in
packing stuff back is awkward
doors and trunks open and slam

Goodbyes and hugs
fuzzy car lights trail out
to the highway
we listen to fading sounds
you start the engine

Bruce England, California, USA

incarnation

snow falling
across the Sahara
at sunset
you give me pink crystals
of ancient desert roses

in the lee
of this sacred mountain
our breath rises
mingling with clouds
until we fall as snow

Debbie Strange, Canada

We Trouble the Donkeys in Saline Valley

We don't see them
the donkeys are somewhere
beyond our camp
we find some weathered bones
cracked white and not taken

Eventually,
everyone leaves the hot springs
and goes to bed
the braying donkeys walk
between the tents to water

Bruce England, California, USA

A Fire Pearl

insatiable thirst . . .
between the scorching days
and the rainy season
the buds of a cactus
don't want yet to open

a fire pearl
in the Japanese garden . . .
the old cactus
after a long waiting
at last is blooming

Vasile Moldovan, Romania

Heatwave

baby bats
died in the heatwave
how many birds
fell off their perches
rivals share the bird bath

all birds wait
while the young butcherbird
quenches its thirst
even the magpie
watches it bathe

Lorne Henry, New South Wales, Australia

Deep Red

setting
my ringtone
to silence
the chirp, chirp, chirp
of sparrow song

sinking
into a deep sleep
the hum
of the central a.c.
seductive

deeper
and deeper into
myself—
the ohm of
a ceiling fan

a deep red
from these street lights
on this cold night
a lone soldier
humming

street lights dot
this empty boulevard—
I slip
in and out
of my shadow

Dave Read, Calgary, Alberta, Canada
Akane, Texas, USA

Six:
Black Umbrella

wreckage

I tried
to make you fall in love
with the sea
but you were never fond
of heavy weather

amidst the flotsam
and jetsam of this life
we salvage
our brightest memories
before they turn to rust

Debbie Strange, Canada

Storms to Come

that cool breeze
is a harbinger
of storms to come:
Earl, Fiona, Gaston
crossing the Atlantic

a tarnished sun
in a glistening sea
a wooden ship
makes her way
towards shelter

a forest
of fishboats
rafted
side by side
in the hurricane hole

sitting in the pew
where Melville sat,
with a hurricane
bearing down on me,
I contemplate the cenotaphs

no denomination
no cross, no stained glass,
just the silence
of marble memories
in Seamen's Bethel

I want
to say something profound
but I'm tired
and slightly worried
about the weather

M. Kei, Seaman's Bethel, New Bedford, Massachusetts, USA

rain, rain

it is no use
going to the village
the road is closed
the water is lapping
at all the doors

the pub is shut
water a foot deep
on the old flagstones
the ale casks bobbing
floating in the cellar

the cows have moved
to higher ground
the Hollow Lane
is busy with rabbits
their meadow flooded

long-ago man built
his churches here
on high places
the water runs downhill
the graves stay dry

I sit in the porch
above waterlogged fields
thinking of Noah
and praying for enough sun
for just one rainbow

Joy McCall, Norfolk, England

The Search

a single iris
looks over the stream
how deep
do I need to look
for my reflection

> *from me*
> *to the bottom of the stream*
> *a blue fire*
> *burns*
> *silently*

Kath Abela Wilson, Pasadena, California, USA
Peggy Castro, Los Angeles, California, USA

Gathering

waiting by the river
floating candles
for the hungry ghosts
a boatman stops on his way
his palms together

killing time
with the hibiscus
I listen about their dew
Is it the warrior in me, paying
homage with sticks and stones

at the peak
of the mountain
looking at a faraway mist
I prostrate, until I am
my own shadow

at the foot
of the mountain
I unclasp the twilight
my robe is too small
to hold the moon

perhaps it's time
to leave my zafu
but the moonlight
through leaves
has not stopped talking

Malintha Perera, Sri Lanka

Nature's Lesson

from the sink
I spot a white flower
under the palm tree
walking irises last one day
so I pluck three to admire

a tall blue vase
white and purple irises
from my garden
I'll enjoy their beauty
they'll die tonight

by morning
irises have shrivelled
the leaves
their long spear shapes
lasting elegance

surprise
a few days later
three irises
face the white ceiling
it's taken years to learn this

Lorne Henry, New South Wales, Australia

autumn rain

where we started
a summer short
with the first plums
on the orchard catwalk
breathing out purple

autumn rain
you going home
with a black umbrella
and someone else's
day of grief

ai li, london, england, and singapore

Sailors

the gutters
are overflowing
the pub is awash
going back to bed
till the rain stops

    two by two
    the sodden sailors
    climb aboard the ship
    for another night of solitaire
    and Spencer Tracey flicks

    Joy McCall, Norwich, England
    Michael H. Lester, Los Angeles, California, USA

Boys

running
through the blades
of dawn
these boys
ahead of me

their faces
no longer appear
in the window—
I shovel
the snow alone

the hours
we used to spend at
the park
we pass without
a glance

he calls
me out for
one-on-one
convinced
this time he'll win

listening
as he plays
piano
better
than I ever did

a balance
between light
and shade—
my youngest son
draws manga

yearning
to find their way
in the world
they still need
me to drive

Dave Read, Alberta, Canada

Snow

the Inuktitut
articulate what
I cannot—
the subtle details
of winter and life

qanittaq:
the layering of snow
and ice
the heaviness of all
these years

piqsirpoq:
drifting snow
I float
unanchored through
my thoughts

sauvaa:
to bury deep
in the snow
all the moments
I've forgotten

maujaq:
the snow into which
one sinks
the resolute
lessening of my days

salittutaq:
snow thinned by
a warm wind
the memories of spring
and love

qannisiutuq:
to journey in snow
preparing
to set out
into my final nights

Marianne Paul, Canada

*Source of Inuktitut words and meanings: The Canadian Encyclopedia, https://
www.historicacanada.ca/blog/30-inuktitut-words-for-snow-and-ice/.*

Two Winters

florida goth
who's never seen snow
wondering if
he's the corpse flower
in the hothouse

in winter
there's no
shame in
the bottle—
only wee

Grunge, Florida, USA

Seven:
Never Will I Return

freefall

we are fledglings
leaping into this world
with open arms
trusting that the sedges
will soften our fall

wood duck hens
remember the place where
they first took flight
home means something
different to us all

Debbie Strange, Canada

What We Shoulder

the heft
of fifty-pound seed sacks
portioned out
by the scoopful
along weathered deck rails

the infinite
black oil seeds that slide
down scrub jay crops
the way incalculable drops
of rain slake a gauge

ironic luck
sunflowers popping up
cache after cache
beak-secreted in the mulch
of manicured landscaping

migrating flocks
we hope we helped launch
the acres
of sun-gilt faces
orbiting on clockwise watch

the blue
of a flight feather lost
borne aloft
amidst petals falling soft
as sunlight on stones

Autumn Noelle Hall, Green Mountain Falls, Colorado, USA

the slant of light

ancestors
I wish I had known them
one and all
or to know just their wishes
the slant of light in their eyes

a tin pot
full of spent matches—
empty oil lamps
the faint smell of smudged wicks
the acrid taste of despair

to blaze
and burn out
like a star
this very earth glimmering
waiting, we watch in wonder

Joy McCall, Norwich, England
Don Wentworth, Pennsylvania, USA

Gleanings

fingers drum
on the table top
impatient
for my explanation
that dent in the car

    thunderheads
    bring rain that hammers
    parched ground . . .
    the farmer puts aside
    his pain and his gun

my father
ploughs in stubble
day on day
the monotony . . .
preparing for planting

    harvest time
    corellas grow fat
    on gleanings —
    the jostle of endless
    diets and recipes

at the silo
heavily laden trucks
in a line
waiting drivers discuss
wheat prices and politics

> *last night*
> *you talked of nothing*
> *but love . . .*
> *was there a grain of truth*
> *in anything you said*

the bin
beside my desk
is overflowing . . .
all your subterfuge,
implausible excuses

Marilyn Humbert, Sydney, NSW, Australia
Laura Davis, Sydney, NSW, Australia

Bearing the Burden

a garden troll
and beautiful flowers
cannot hide the outrage
a black snake weaving
through the chipmunk den

in the pond gone silent
a bullfrog's pain-torn croaks
a snake swallowing its leg . . .
to protest the laws of nature
I thrash the water with a stick

releasing the goat's horns
from the barbwire fence . . .
musk on my hands
blood on my shoe
I bear the burden home

Elizabeth Howard, Tennessee, USA

Homestead

The idle school bus fading yellow into windswept grass. Surveying the muddied strut of barnyard hens, the freeholder lifts a sorry hand from behind the newspapered windows of old number thirty-two. Waves through the windshield to his few neighbors now departing.

abiding in
the transient
a home
cobbled alone
from memory

The old house nearby has collapsed in upon itself. Murky panes shattered, grey wood splintered. Lace curtains billow from a gutted parlor. A cur growls from the shadow of his own ramshackle dwelling. It better preserved than the other. Yet both now in danger of true oblivion.

KEEP OUT signs
from the wildfire
embers settling
along the dirt track
he refuses to travel

Matthew Caretti, Ha Lumisi, Lesotho

Cast Out

I drove
down the country lane
to where
my great-grandparents
had settled in 1850

I could see
the old house still standing
on a high point
swept around by the river
what a superb site

accosted
by an American
who proclaimed
you are trespassing
be on your way

Lorne Henry, New South Wales, Australia

ruined

the croft
has fallen to ruin
the west wind
has stolen the roof thatch
there is no shelter here

the cupboard doors
are all broken
thieves have stolen
the china cups
and the silver spoons

the chimney
is blocked with birds' nests
the logs in the pile are rotten
we will light our fires
of driftwood and seaweed

the bedding
is mildewed and dank
the well is running
clear and cold
there is water to drink

I am home
I search myself for signs
of the life that was mine
the house, my self—all the same
we are broken and torn

Joy McCall, inner lands

Bitter Spring

I don't know why
an old-timer named it bitter,
why the name stuck,
yet it's called bitter
to this day

the source of the spring
appears to be a face
an ancient bearded man,
though it's only a stone
covered with moss

a gnarled cedar
overhangs the spring,
a timeworn cup
hanging on a stob
waiting . . .

I take it in my hands
fill it, sip a few drops . . .
it's earthy, as if it surged up
from the earth's depths,
gathering flavors as it rose

the detritus of prehistory,
soil where dinosaurs
feasted and fought—
slobber, afterbirth, blood,
body waste intermingled

soil from the age
when man lived in caves,
ate roots, sprouts,
planted the first
rudimentary garden

soil from the first city,
built by men for the Man
who would be king,
his brothers serving
his every whim

soil from wars
that decimated the earth
brother killing brother,
killing mother, child,
and preborn

I would return the cup
to the cedar stob
and go my way
hoping to forget this spring,
bitter indeed

but I seem to hear a voice,
a deep hollow voice—
is it the voice of the stone face?
I trace the tears spilling down
the wasted cheeks for eons

you cannot run from
what you have seen and heard
take the cup and care for it,
you will forever drink
this cup of bitterness

Elizabeth Howard, Tennessee, USA

Dakota Survivor: Grand Forks, ND 1947– 1964

a pilgrimage
surveying the prairie
from a
'63 Plymouth
running 90 mph

on the face
of every resident
a fog
I learned to break free from
by emigrating

he laughed
and called it fun
at his end
of the bullwhip
thrashing me

not hard
to impress them
small town
celebrity and fame
of no account

wading
through bullrushes
of the coulee
outside the city
the pop-pop of a BB gun

my weakness
plagued me city-wide
at every turn
where today's strength
came from I know not

my muse
was both a mask
and
my redeeming self
spinning out melodies

never again
will I return to that
place of agony
a hometown that was
never my home

Richard St. Clair, North Dakota, USA

Eight:
The Boulder I Can't Move

Passed By

smoking opium
in an empty park—
my boyhood
passed by
running fast

> *getting high*
> *and higher*
> *yet*
> *my girlfriend*
> *on the swings*

outside
dark rain falling—
400 yen
for a fragrant rose
but you'll never know

> *the brittle*
> *life of a lilac*
> *bush—*
> *the air the scent of*
> *late May snow*

in shadows
showering
for work
afternoon heat curves
over dead grass

Akane, Texas, USA
Dave Read, Calgary, Alberta, Canada

Unable to Sleep

Eyes open at night
a weight on my chest gets up
jumps off edge of bed
thinking cannot move my arms
my eyes down from the ceiling

Along the bed
an invisible presence
moves in front of me
my sheets slide down, my body
slides down, I fall on the floor

Struggling in the sheets
jerking my arms off my chest
bolt upright, awake,
shaking, peering into dark,
back down, unable to sleep

Bruce England, California, USA

West Park, Florida

There was a kid that lived next door to my grandparents. He'd always try to climb the fence. It didn't have barbed wire, but it was one of those chain link fences with the sharp prongs on top. I always figured he'd get punctured on that fence. I didn't figure it'd be a bullet that got him.

wild-eyed toddler
staring at the big kids
through the fence —
stray bullet deciding
we'd never get to play

Grunge, Florida, USA

Weather Report

scanning your face
for today's mood
I launch out
on conversational seas
alert for dangerous rips

> *isobars*
> *on the weather map*
> *lying close*
> *we generate*
> *a cyclone of turbulence*

dangerous winds
are stirring the air
at this party
I pay careful attention
to the hum of ambition

> *a wasp*
> *from the wild buzzes*
> *through the open door*
> *the hilltops under cloud*
> *look closer than my dreams*

a noisy party
finally shuts down next door —
the celebration
continues without them
. . . surround sound of cicadas

on the surges
of your snoring
I dream
I'm sailing
into a king tide

Jan Foster, Australia
Anne Benjamin, Australia

Tangled Roots

as rootless
as an aerophyte[1]
in a vacuum
the threads of my life nothing
but a matted ball of lint

how ruthlessly
loose ends are bound up
and discarded—
his yell as loud
as the vacuum cleaner

Tamara K. Walker, Colorado, USA

[1] *aerophyte Plant that derives moisture and nutrients from the air and rain; usually grows on another plant but not parasitic on it.*

Vocabulary.com. 2017. <https://www.vocabulary.com/dictionary>

Ladybird

the house with girls
is always locked . . .
a ladybird
ignoring the padlock enters
and comes out when it wants

this ladybird
undecided as me . . .
after a while
if I ignore it
will fly to nowhere

Vasile Moldovan, Romania

Even the Dust Will Speak

she is neither murderer
nor thief, but scholar
with a forbidden book,
a visionary dreaming
of freedom for women

masked, she stands in the dust
before the drawn sword
they expect her to cry out
but she will go down in silence . . .
even the dust will speak for her

Elizabeth Howard, Tennessee, USA

riverstone

following
his announcement
a calm
with where the title
leads

emerging
from out of
a random pile
grasping his call
with two hands

balancing
two
on
one
the therapy of
stacking
stones

Don Miller, New Mexico, USA

the last rose

I didn't know you were
a childhood sexual abuse survivor
until that time we . . .
you threw up
I felt so helpless

if I let go
the whole world
will fall to pieces . . .
shattered
snow globe

"Everything's fine here."
— broken bottles
— broken bones
"We're doing well."
— blackouts

the last rose
you gave me
so brittle
around the edges
of my heart

years later
I realize
I am a survivor too . . .
cigarette burns
on crocheted lace

clinging
to the ceiling
after his advances —
the first time I remember
leaving my body

today the world
is too big
to contemplate
I hide under a blanket
with my dog

autumn sky —
the stars have drifted
far from home . . .
beneath my eyes
deep shadows

two halves
of my brain
at war . . .
I choose the side
without migraines

I still dream
about you
drowning . . .
a high water mark
on the brick wall

someday
I hope to think
of you without
survivor's guilt—
flash migraine

reunified
I find my inner child
by the ocean—
driftwood arms full
of seaweed blankets

Julie Bloss Kelsey, Maryland, USA

Hawthorne Hedges

onward
though the thorns sting
and the brambles bite —
the light breaks through
the thickets that hold us

    from seed
    to adolescent shrub
    we feed
    our beloved hawthorn hedges
    despite their prickly thorns

Joy McCall, Norwich, England
Michael H. Lester, Los Angeles, California, USA

Becoming

a boulder
I can't move
what do I do
when you always
think you're right

Susan Burch, Maryland, United States

wind and rain
tossed into the river
I feel my way
between floating
and sinking

Jessica Malone Latham, Santa Rosa, California, USA

taking her life back
piece by piece
a robin builds its nest
surrendering to this moment
petals float to the sky

Mary Hohlman, Northern California, USA

watching
the flames rise
and fall into ashes
I remake myself
summer phoenix

Christina Sng, Singapore

thunder rattles
each window pane
you ask
when I learned
to fight back

Tiffany Shaw-Diaz, United States

a labyrinth —
this part in me
that no one knows
I spiral into the core
of my freedom

Josie Hibbing, The Philippines

Lightning Strikes

lightning strikes
unnoticed —
last coffee
with a friend
heading east

Borges talks,
flaneur walks . . .
you left me
somewhere
in the labyrinth

in a visceral state
going in circles,
sometimes literally . . .
free advice,
but chained to chemicals

birds heard,
but not felt . . .
walking the inclement
night sedated
by sleeping pills

shifting objects
in the dust
until chemicals
in the eyes . . .
blanket on the window

too afraid
to phone the crisis line . . .
I wanted
to ask them
for a Coke

in the psych unit
another patient tells me
I don't deserve to eat . . .
the room spinning,
nurses passing by

just going
from spot to spot . . .
sea
    sickness
on the psych

a nurse tells me
you got to do something . . .
Kind of Blue
Miles Davis
over and over

setting a discharge date—
a nurse tells me
there still might
be hope
for me

shaving my beard,
taking a shower—
picking up
a book
I read before

Marshall Bood, Saskatchewan, Canada

Nine:
Sacred Sites

the fox and the sandman

the day is flying
the skies are dark
it's suppertime
in old Norwich
the sandman is calling

    skirting
    the wrenched geometry
    cast by the cabin's
    yellow window-light
    a fox passes on silent paws

    Joy McCall, Norwich, England
    Larry Kimmel, Massachusetts, USA

Zazenkai

plum-dyed leaves,
I forget the path
going off
going off
to the village

staff in hand
my shadow waves
at the cotton clouds
only the wind follows me
to my cloaked wooden bed

how have I
misled the bees
the butterflies
brush my tilted hat
and one is on my shoulder

caught
In the sudden rain
I shelter
the ripe berries
to be offered to the Buddhas

Malintha Perera, Sri Lanka

spectral

in the space
between wakefulness
and dreaming
my sister sings songs
I have yet to write

my dreamscapes
haunted by green spirals
of aurora
these memories of you
conjured out of light

last night
I dreamt of things
fantastical
this morning, my life
so dull and drear

night after night
this recurring dream
the universe
is telling me something
I do not understand

Debbie Strange, Canada

dream tanka

mirror lake
the widowed swan
gliding on
its
own reflection

an owl
under
another full moon
calling out
to my loneliness

my youth
is hiding
in
this mirror
bathed in candlelight

careless whisper
speaking
to the leaves
before winter
takes hold

a lone skater
scratching
all my dreams
within
your ice palace

ai li, london, england, and singapore

Crucible

New diagnosis;
Psoriatic arthritis.
In the march of time,
The milestones gradually
Come to resemble tombstones.

One day waking up,
Knowing it down to the bone
That help is needed.
Giving yourself permission
To find a way to survive.

It's not that the world
Suddenly got so much worse.
Sometimes we wake up,
See some of the suffering,
And can't believe it's normal.

Emotions are real
The same as hunger and thirst
And the need to sleep.
It's ok to care for them
As you would anything else.

The anxiety
Insists the nightmares are real,
That things are hopeless,
And that nothing can be done,
And it's hard to disagree.

On feeling better:
Moving past the unlit lands,
Gratitude to all
Those hearts that offered shelter;
There but for their grace go I.

Off to the doctor
To make a blood sacrifice,
So they can divine
If the pills that save the bones
Are destroying the organs.

It's hard not to hear
When that little voice within
Says that you're a fool.
It's hard to keep on going
When all it says is to stop.

Then a friend points out
That maybe being a fool
Is the very thing,
And suddenly there's a smile
Because it's alright to be.

Trying to be strong
And all the while wondering
Just how long until
Psoriatic arthritis
Turns me into a cripple.

Filling the empty,
But starting to ask questions.
What is it for and
Why try to be rid of it?
It's always been there for me.

The sense of pressure;
It becomes overwhelming.
The clock is staring;
It's judging every minute,
And it's never satisfied.

Keep a quiet love;
The world only gets harder.
Keep it safe inside,
Just the way you did before
You knew it would be like this.

You'll do great today.
Just stand up and keep moving.
Don't let you stop you.
It's not as impossible
As you tell yourself it is.

All that we can do
To make sense out of our lives
Is to describe them,
But don't mistake description
As being the thing itself.

Christopher Shawn Rathburn, Minnesota, USA

While Running the Course

The thoughts of the earth are my thoughts

this grandmother body
stretching before a 10k
in my hometown
the hospital where I was born
crumbled long ago

to raise money
for church youth to help the homeless
read the post;
did I sign up
only to clock my pace?

The voice of the earth is my voice

the starting horn
at predetermined intervals;
my iPod
dies unexpectedly
before the second mile

my lucky socks
breathe,
breathe I say
passing the resting place
of dead relatives

All that belongs to the earth belong to me

orange cones
in the middle of the road
unevenly spaced
my stride
on this cold spring pavement

unzipping my jacket,
knotting it around my waist
how refreshing
this water
water from these young church volunteers!

All that surrounds the earth surrounds me

to a stranger
I toss my jacket, my keys
before crossing
hardened steel —
the railroad's parallel lines

where the road curves
and overlooks the Grand River
an eagle
lends me
her DNA

It is lovely indeed; it is lovely indeed.

Tish Davis, Painesville, Ohio

Italics: American Indian. "Navajo Song." <*www.world prayers.org/archives/
prayers/celebrations/it_is_lovely_indeed*>.

Dancing Through It All

an earthquake jolt
power still out
realizing
I'm not prepared
to rebuild my life

> *our unstable world—*
> I'm standing
> on a sea of fishes—
> *an ancient poet described*
> *exactly how I feel now*

oceans warmer
coral dying off
we've infected our planet . . .
don't have a drug
to cure it

> *out to the garden*
> *the thrust and heave of a spade*
> *in winter-wet clay*
> *my clasp knife not strong enough*
> *to cut out the rot we've made*

my trans granddaughter
ten years old
claps and stomps the beat
around the kitchen
how can I nurture her future?

I'd like to teach her
my beautiful granddaughter
what I couldn't do
to keep on dancing
even if there's no applause

David Rice, Berkeley, California, USA
Lynne Leach, California, USA

Sacred Sites

"Instead of calling on some scholar I paid many a visit to particular trees. These were shrines I visited both winter and summer."

Henry David Thoreau

spring grass
brilliant with light
resplendent
these are days
when anything can happen

Sakura dreams begin in early April when all of Japan is delighted, out in nature enjoying yamazakura—wild mountain cherry trees in bloom. In parks, temple and shrine gardens appears a first wave of trees veiled in pale pink blossoms, from the island of Kyushu in the South their progress announced on the daily news. Gradually moving in waves North to Kyoto and Tokyo, all the way to Hokkaido. Exciting weeks in all the land when friends meet, families gather to picnic and drink sake and green tea, with tales, songs and ancient dances under cherry trees. The wind scatters petals into tea bowls of freshly whisked matcha, into boxes of sushi and sakura-mochi sweets. It is a time of awakening after winter.

a child's top
spinning through time-space
comes to rest
ready to be spun
by another hand

This is the season each year when I feel a pleasant nostalgia remembering life in Tokyo and Kyoto, longing to see the venerable trees in bloom. One evening in Kyoto stands out, at a temple at dusk where the first cherry tree to bloom was lit by a light artist in the temple grounds. We were enchanted by the sight of the tree, walked uphill where a teahouse was open to guests — each year I dream of going to Arashiyama, Kiyomizu-dera, the Hoshino mountains to walk and to take a boat along the river. One of these years I will go back.

the willow
weaves a spring tale
this face
without a mirror
petals in the breeze

I wave from
the height of Karatsu castle
to my friends
their smiling faces raised
among the scent of sakura

*   *   *

in Tibet we venture out early
to visit the marketplace
walking an alley
full of one-room shops
owners cross-legged outside

The beggars are jostling tourists in the Bakhor Bazaar. All the clothes of an empty city strung on poles and awnings. On trestle tables a litter of radios, plastic toys, miniature Buddhas, tinkling bells and incense. Woven carpets for sale lie gathering dust on the roadside. A ragged old woman ties a sheep to a railing, her hands quick and reptilian. Our feet slap on cobblestones, as we walk around groups of monks and Tibetan herdsmen, clothed from head to foot in animal skins. The beggars scatter.

> market day—
> a small hand-bell
> at the monastery
> summons monks to prayer,
> their chants rhythmic in the air

> under the spell
> of vendors in the square
> we become wallflowers
> watching from the wings
> as they sell aphrodisiacs

Their hidden language echoes in the hollow walls, their faces unseen, muffled in scarves. The bells ring for prayer. Soon everyone returns to their business. Perhaps it's real and not a stage set. A vendor's radio clangs like old pipes. We wander to a bookshop where we hope to buy a book of poetry. Most of the books I can't read: the language sings its secrets beyond my eyes and ears. I trace the shape of words, listen to the Tibetan guide as she reads poems I can't understand, woven with a fine thread, painted with a sable brush, carved in marble. I sound the words ineffectively, but their beauty remains with me.

> joining pilgrims
> on a spiritual stroll
> around centuries-old
> stupas and monasteries
> prayer flags fluttering

far into the evening
we wander hidden
backstreet shrines
and learn about sublime
temple art and Buddhas

Giselle Maya, France
Patricia Prime, New Zealand

Moab Mandala*

ancient glyph
the humanoid form
of our lives
taking shape in
each shared moment

ephemeral pool
somewhere between
the rich sediment
and blue sky surface
my reflection

half moon sky
in the beginning
an intention
to grow into
that which is

forgotten cairn
a gnarled juniper
tells the story
of some lost traveler
seeking grace

paired ravens
desire and memory
ride thermals
from the river below
to touch moab rim

* *"Mandala is a Sanskrit word that works to connect the ideas of center and periphery, or center and fringe. While mandalas are often associated with two-dimensional Tibetan diagrams used as an aid in visualization practice, in general, a mandala is the unification of many vast elements into one view through the experience of meditation. Seeming complexity and chaos are simplified into a pattern and natural hierarchy."*

~Chögyam Trungpa Rinpoche

Matthew Caretti, Ha Lumisi, Lesotho

Ten:
Wild Swans

Chasing Wonderland

the *Stephen Tabor**
creaks at its rising dock
we wanna-be crew
scramble aboard for the week
with bulging duffel bags

Maine's chill
deepens with night . . .
bundled
in my bunk with a mild cold
on-deck sea chanties lull me

one working head
for five men, eight women . . .
at rush times
we try counting clouds
'til it's our turn to unzip

a southeast breeze
blows us past wooded islands
the newbies
learn a sheet isn't a rope
and fore is the 'pointy part'

one pan
of warm water each morning
we wash
our selective stinky parts
hope cold air blows off the rest

my small sailboat
would fit the *Tabor's* galley
only in dreams
had I scattered Maine waters,
mast nearly touching the sun

three of us
are trusted to take the wheel
come about, I order
my weight dangling from a spoke
to force the bow through wind's wall

fog hits
and we ghost along
I'm sure I hear
the *Tabor's* first crew
moan at every buoy

at anchor
for the evening and fed
I sit bundled up
watch sunset paint the sky,
heart swelling with wonder

it's our last morning
before this trek comes to an end
saddened, two of us
skim the two-oared dinghy
once more over deep green

engineless,
a motored dink pushes us
to dock —
clothes rumpled and nose burnt
it feels like I'm leaving home

Pris Campbell, Maine, USA

* Launched in 1871, the 68 foot Steven Tabor is the oldest documented schooner in the U.S.

One Day at Point Pinos Lighthouse: A Docent's Reflection and Refraction

The purpose of the docent is to increase public awareness of the historical importance of the Point Pinos Lighthouse, its architecture, its function, and its surrounding natural history.
—Lighthouse Docent Position Description (City of Pacific Grove, California)

Westward is Point Pinos with the lighthouse in a wilderness of sand where you will find the lighthouse keeper playing at the piano and making ship models . . . and with a dozen other elegant pursuits and interests . . .
—lighthouse placard to record his visit with lighthouse keeper Allen Luce (Robert Louis Stevenson, 1879)

after five years
as a hospice volunteer
I think it is time
for something less dark—
I know . . . a lighthouse docent

at the entrance
low-lying sagewort sway
not with the wind
but of their own volition—
it's time to unlock the gate

I watch the tide
surge out of Monterey Bay—
past the bell buoy
I think I can see China
in the foggy morning

high winds today
in a Coast Guard cutter's tow
past our lighthouse
the schooner, *Reliance*—
"the sea, She be rough!"

our Fresnel lens
sends a beam 17 miles—
I ask a visitor
if she had come far
her response: "It all depends."

time for a breather—
from the upstairs bedroom
I watch gulls following
a fishing boat heading home
it must have been a good catch

it's a clean sweep
sand on the spiral staircase
coins in the jar
deposits left behind—
docents close up the lighthouse

Neal Whitman, Pacific Grove, California, USA

Sebastian

The hungry man can't read his timepiece on the nightstand because there's a glare on its crystal face. His reflection in the window doesn't help but it feels like way past dinnertime for sure. The split-pea soup in the freezer sounds good but it took a long time to grow those peas and make the soup. Instead he decides the time is right to write another letter or perhaps a simple poem . . .

> Sun fades
> into a maroon splash
> on the western horizon . . .
> you slowly curl up
> into the song of night.

There's no forgetting you, my fingers running through your hair, your nose against my cheek. We've howled together at the moon and taken in the starlight. We've watched the waves roll on the shore. We've walked across the field. We've wallowed in the mudflats and we've crossed the street together . . .

> If I gave you a bone
> to chew
> you'd chew it . . .
> thanks for keeping
> our secrets.

Richard Grahn, Maquoit Bay, Brunswick, Maine, USA

A Tribute

She always held life by the reins. Elegantly matching outfits, making the perfect cup of tea, designing a business plan or holding a dinner party—nothing was ever good enough, until excellence had been achieved in her eyes. Fitness, tennis, gardening, gourmet cooking—she did it all with charm, grace and British style.

> two old friends
> one brain tumour
> after the news
> I walk beside
> a river of tears

Help her across the street when you take her out, her husband said. If she starts to have a seizure, find this pill in her pocket, and get it under her tongue. Be careful, though, she bites.

> her fingers
> entwined in mine
> this walk
> around the block
> a marathon now

Don't talk about her illness, he said. Don't ask about her medication or the next operation.

> to hell with
> the elephant
> in the room—
> I can still make
> her laugh

She loved music, especially opera. I had never been to an opera, so she took me to a series of shows. We sat in the gods, our winter coats stuffed behind the last row of seats.

no goodbyes
just that look
in her eye—
at home I listen to
la traviata

Only sixty-one. But enough time to love her husband, raise two sons, enchant her friends and enhance her community. Enough time for a complete symphony, written on her terms, without compromise.

she was radiant
in fall colours
at the cemetery
the trees
pay tribute

Leslie Bamford, Ontario, Canada

From Wikipedia: The gods (UK English) is a theatrical term, referring to the highest areas of a theatre such as the upper balconies. These are generally the cheapest seats. One reason for naming the cheapest seats "the gods" is because the theatres have beautifully painted ceilings, often mythological themes, so the cheap seats are up near the gods. Another is that those seated in "the gods" look down upon both the performers and the occupants of more expensive seats, like the Olympian Gods looking down from Mount Olympus upon the lives of mortal people.

Sequence #2

ice turns to slush
back to ice
returns to slush
March cloudy day
daffodils forecasted

> *old letters*
> *and diaries . . . the wind*
> *has archived*
> *tumbleweed*
> *against the barbed wire fence*

pink and blue
marshmallow chicks
still in wrappings
yellow ones
nowhere to be found

> *wings tattooed*
> *on his shoulder blades*
> *the aerialist*
> *tells the child not*
> *to fly too near the sun*

in Yellowstone
the bison bull cuts
our path off
between the herds —
long way round

bamboo forest
mountainside canopy
the samurai sits
silent, still, cross-legged
ready to fight

in his bombed
living room
the Syrian man enjoys
Mozart's Oboe Concerto
on his record player

the potter's hands
wheel turning void
cup of green tea
cools
on the window sill

clay Buddha melts
in the rain
playground bully
meets
his match

a wave erases
my footprints
I keep walking
as if I could reach
that horizon

Michael G. Smith, United States
Miriam Sagan, United States

Bitter Stacks

I read
about the Holocaust,
yet how much suffering
still exists in
today's world

wherever I go,
here or there,
this world
remains
a terrible place

the day is long
reading about
survivors
I cannot escape
the terror

Sanford Goldstein, Shibata-shi, Japan

Close to Home

I have stared out
through this window many times
who knows the sum
of such idleness
or is it inspiration?

I stood there this morning
a fresh cup of coffee
sending its aroma
from the table beside me
into the autumn air

alone in the house
cradling a cooling cup
pen and paper
lie in wait for me
like some hungry beast

Here, after all, was time. A time recalled from the depths
of memory. London had been bombed beyond recognition,
but the people lifted themselves up and began to rebuild
their homes and their lives all over again. The world carried
on peacefully after the grip of war and my father's return
from Germany. I hardly recognised him in his uniform as he
lay his kit-bag in the front room of our terraced house. He
took items from it like a magician: china dolls for me and
my sisters, metal cars and a jeep for my brothers, a handbag
for my mother. Soon, life settled down and the struggle
began for people to build a new order out of the rubble of
the destroyed past.

At night, in summer while my parents read the newspaper, a hot wind might come from the south and if I went out with friends to the cinema or to a dance, we would look at the stars across a million miles. We might even hear a faint sound from space. Sometimes we'd see a shooting star or the moon sailing in the sky, casting its light on the dark streets. The city lay silent in the moonlight. Above us the moon and stars went on their magical courses and then the sun rose into the silence.

*   *   *

recovering
from a snowstorm
chill puddles
snow-patched fields —
an earth-sheltered life

how do trees survive
days and nights of snow
and ice
blossoms wait to breathe the sky
a tentative dream . . .

The story of post-war hardships seems effaced in the volcanic fires of the earth's centre — they are so painful that they no longer seem real. Father did not go to war, instead made a splendid garden, so our family could eat. He turned the radio on and said out loud: "Who would listen to this nonsense . . ." and changing the station to Mozart or Chopin, started to hum along.

We were evacuated to the country where my aunt lived with her family on a farm in a small village. It was there I fell in love with the countryside, forests, meadows, streams where mother and I picked watercress and where I lost my favourite book "Thumbelina" in the long grass—we could not find it again. My brother had to stop going to school when there were air attacks as the train he had to take came to a halt, passengers hid under the train and school was suspended. It was then he taught me the Greek alphabet and asked me to recite it for visitors.

Vaguely I recall air raids where we had to dash to subterranean shelters for the night. Once we picked ears of wheat at harvest time when a plane swooped down on us— we hid in deep ditches. These nearly effaced nightmares— did they really happen? They did. And even now in other lands they do. So many years later now, I have created a peaceful life, to garden as my father did, read as mother loved to do, to write and paint, with much work to be done every day.

releasing its hold
this long harsh winter
I am ready
to be embraced
by scented breezes

deep in the garden soil
where the toad hibernates
soon to emerge
among blue periwinkles
and shady rhubarb leaves

Patricia Prime, New Zealand
Giselle Maya, France

time to quit

I have seen
the best meter maids
of my generation
retire
and go on medicaid

> *the traffic warden*
> *leans on the wall*
> *in the sunshine*
> *singing "que será será"*
> *walking stick at his side*

Larry Kimmel, Massachusetts, USA
Joy McCall, Norwich, England

Keeping My Promise

there are many reasons
not to buy a puppy
when you are seventy —
I did not know
any of them

my garden of
roses and phlox
a puppy's playground
I will plant dogwood
next spring

wearing Ralph Lauren
to the leash-free park
I hope the dogs
appreciate
my outfit

an old soul lives in
our puppy
his brown eyes
rejuvenating
my aging years

sit — leave it —
lie down — walk away
dog commands make
good advice for
humans too

the dog shows me
a drowning butterfly
I scoop it up
from the water
playing God

taking photographs
while the dog
hunts for frogs
our morning break from
the hands of time

dressing for dinner
was once slinky black
now it means
taking off my long johns
while the dog sleeps

after the dog fight
I take my wounds
to bed—
my feelings hurt
more than my leg

giving up on housework
to write a tanka
in the sunroom
a snoring dog
is oddly soothing

inventing a game
and playing it often
my canine Edison
wrestles the pillow
into submission

stroking his head
I gaze into
those brown eyes
gateway to
another realm

a young dog
and me
growing old
I grab the leash
keep my promise

Leslie Bamford, Ontario, Canada

wild swans : a dream-poem

the asphalt road goes on, grey, long, here straight, there a curve: Janus has turned his head, time has shifted like pebbles on a shore, as the tide goes out, comes in: it is a new year, winter, a January of mists and pervasive frosts, a needle of wind with its cutting point: the gulls sound like some raw, raucous chorale, I can see the trees at the foot of the slow hill, a winter sun sensational and cold and white like the wings of the gulls as they go and glide through the whitening sky, spirit-birds, free as the wind, implacable, riding the air, gliding over the rime, the frosty morning as a wonder of tree and bush and theatre, when the world flows over the brim with light in the fibre of the wild . . .

poetry is just a paper dream—a butterfly, and the butterflies are now just part of our dreams, the prophecies of spring with its floral ballet, the mind's own exuberance and flow, songbirds in their sung flow singing like water, nature's woven fabric, its tongue, its leaves and foliage like flame over the ancient well with its deep experiences, the spring, the spring, the breaking of time and ground with new life, weeks away, weeks ahead, the hope of our lives to come, to be, and to bud, and to grow, flowers of light, the sun, the snowdrop, the daffodil in March, the season of butterfly and wing and the colours of the mind in this great dialectics, or dispensation . . .

months of working in a library, an old gormenghast of a building in sequences of old rooms, which housed ancient collections of books, scriptures, Mozarabic Bibles, volumes in Hebrew, Latin and Greek, books on church history, archaeology, the Dead Sea Scrolls, the writings of the fathers, the old hermits, the saints, and then all those similar wisdoms in Hindu, Buddhist, Islamic and Baha'i texts, all the philosophies of Greece, all the comparisons and structures of myths, the mythologies of time, eras, mouths, minds, evolutions, and moods, that slow still pool of knowledge, the ancient trees, leaves, the spring of enlightenment, the coming of stars in the morning, journeys, transformations, light, and all the dust of the world on shelves of heavy books, the hands that reached for them, the ink, the eyes, the scripts of old and almost forgotten tongues, cuneiform writing on five-thousand-year-old bricks . . .

and the sudden metamorphosis of the moment, the urge to shape life and go, to be reborn, to emerge from the womb of these chambers, in the loosening of time, the coming of fresh green meditations, a surge of green shoots in my thoughts, a latent pink blossom from bud and branch, blossom that flows now with petal and a bloom rooted in a sudden new world . . .

I walk a path from that library of babel, as if through an orange Shinto gateway (the womb of nature or the womb of the universe), out into this transfiguration of the ground, the hours sublime, speaking now in tongues of water-lilies, flowers that rise out of muck, in the flourishing, the scattering of colour, the iris blue as the sea as it rises over stone, the path grey, here straight, there a curve, taking me down over broken ground, the way rough to the foot, sharp stones shifting, uneven pebble and soil, and moments of Zen, moments of stone, the setting of the stones, leading me on to the morning of my life, down into the grit of the hill, past a mulberry tree, a golden rain tree, a silver birch, some apple trees, down a lavender path, a way that looks over the earth and down to the pond, the river beyond, the river's generated rhythms, as it sings of the sun, a mercurial river, all the world here and present in the grip of the real, absolute, an ovation of joy, peace and wild and breezes, the scent of the moon in the lily, the touch of God in the reed as it greens the pond with new growth . . .

~2~

there are violets growing and quivering like atmosphere, a mineral land that rises like beech trees into the sky: it is the river's raw discipline, the river's many voices and cascades: I walk in the nature of light, the glowing of God in these moments now, as I come here to celebrate the earth and the presence, to be free as those gulls in the gliding wind, the canticle and structure of light, and the lavish winds that are green as the grass that ripples like water through the mind . . .

and here now I come to the river, that is within and without, and follow the river into spring, the river's sequences, its possibilities, its intrinsic music and currency, river of perpetual becoming, of perpetual innovation, and I hear the wings of swans, and the wing of time now becomes light and white, as they erupt like light from the shadow, and the swans open and beat their wings, huge and white as the sun, as the river now comes to life:

swans on
white gospel water —
the freedom
of
their glide . . .

and they will always be balletic in the morning, and they dance like lovers courting, entwine their necks together and miracle the moment as they gather their wings, almost immortally, and beat the air with dreams and symmetry, extend their wings into a morning curved as though time itself were curving, and lift their heads: and they seem held, in their own mysterious beauty, their flow on the water, as in some lines by Yeats, feathers like bright dreaming . . .

and I sing in some ancient chorale, or spell, as if I were singing the land into existence, chanting the green songs, making wishes in that magical time, the white swans lifting now from the waters, powering their white wings like winds, and taking me deep into distant skies, with their ballet and moving and sublime and their wild, their declaration of spring:

the sun at last:
winter fades
into
the flight
of swans

their wings wilder and wilder . . .

A. A. Marcoff, Leatherhead, in the Mole Valley, England

lightfall

black swans
softening the edges
of my darkness
I gather threads of light
unspooling in their wake

the green curl
of a rolling wave
enfolds me
at this tunnel's end
an amazement of light

long after
my time of drowning
I remember
sea anemones
winnowing the light

Debbie Strange, Canada

Contributor Biographies

Contributor Biographies

A. A. Marcoff—Tony is an Anglo-Russian poet, born in Iran, and has lived in Africa, France, Iran and Japan. He has been a university library assistant, a teacher, and has been in charge of poetry and creative writing in a large psychiatric hospital. A main-stream poet as well as a tanka poet, he has been widely published in journals such as 'Poetry Review'. He now lives near the beautiful River Mole.

ai li is a Straits Chinese short form poet from London and Singapore who writes about Life, Love and Loss bringing healing and prayer to her poems. The creator of cherita, editor and publisher of thecherita, founding editor and publisher of still, moving into breath and dew-on-line, she is also an evidential spiritualist medium, an urban photographer, and a surrealist collage painter. Find her essence in the quiet of her inner rooms at: https://www.amazon.com/ai-li/e/B0080X6ROC/ref=sr_tc_2_0?qid=1469884842&sr=1-2-ent.

Akane enjoys both the immediacy and lasting resonance of English language short verse. Akane lives in Texas, USA.

Amelia Fielden is an Australian and her work is based on her life and experiences in Australia. At the same time her tanka are strongly influenced by her work as a translator of Japanese literature and the large amount of time she has spent in Japan.

Anne Benjamin writes poetry, fiction and non-fiction that has appeared in international publications. In 2016, she edited Gemstones, a collection of tanka sequences written in collaboration with poets from Canada, UK, New Zealand and Australia, and published by *Skylark*. The same year, her memoir, of living in India, *Saffron and Silk*, was also published. Anne lives in Sydney, Australia.

Autumn Noelle Hall watches the world from a small cedar cabin on the slopes of Pikes Peak, attempting to make sense of life's senselessness through her writing. She's grateful to the sun for rising each day, to her husband and the mountain's wild creatures for keeping her company, and to all those who so generously read and publish her work. She sincerely hopes it is possible to save the Earth one tanka at a time.

The **Banyan Tree Poets** is an online writing group brought together by a common interest in the Japanese short forms of poetry. Across continents and cultures, participants share a passion for the beauty and subtlety of language, and the value of mutual support and friendship.

They delight in the variety of their pursuits and poetic expressions, always learning from each other.

Barbara Hay is an award-winning children's author and internationally published haiku poet. She is widowed with four children and three grandchildren. Haiku has had a transformative effect on her life and being a member of the Banyan Tree Poets is a large part of that. She was recently appointed as Southwest Regional Coordinator for Haiku Society of America. She lives in Tulsa, Oklahoma. www.barbarahay.com

Billy Simms is an artist, poet, and educator. He lives in Hamilton, OH, with his wife and four cats.

Bruce England lives in Santa Clara and works in San Jose, California as a public librarian. Retirement is planned for late 2018. In some years after that, he will cash out of Silicon Valley for a place to be determined. Publication in tanka anthologies includes: *Fire Pearls 2* (2013), *Bright Stars* (2014), *Neon Graffiti* (2016), and *Earth: Our Common Ground* (2017). Also publication in various anthologies edited by Robert Epstein with tanka includes: *Now This* (2013), *The Sacred in Contemporary Haiku* (2014), *Beyond The Grave* (2015), *Every Chicken, Cow, Fish and Frog* (2016), and *They Gave Us Life* (2017).

Christina Sng (Singapore) is a poet, writer, and artist. She is the author of two haiku collections, *A Constellation of Songs* (Origami Poems Project, 2016) and *Catku* (Allegra Press, 2016). In the moments in between, she finds joy in tending to her herb and bonsai garden. Visit her at christinasng.com.

Christine White enjoys writing creative non-fiction, personal essay, and poetry, as well as song lyrics for her singer/songwriter son Dion. She lives in Kitchener, Ontario, Canada, near her daughter and son-in-law, and her grandchildren. Christine holds a BA degree in Speech Communication.

About the author, **Christopher Shawn Rathburn,** is a licensed clinical psychologist with a history of chronic depression and anxiety, a student of the process of change from both sides of the therapeutic relationship. Currently not in practice, with the support of an amazing wife, he has been writing like his life depends on it. Probably, it does. He lives in the city of Minneapolis, in the state of Minnesota, in the United States of America.

Reclusive suburban writer **dalton perry** resides in Southern California, he began writing poetry in grade school and has been very content with the success of the work he has submitted.

Dave Read is a Canadian poet living in Calgary. He primarily writes short poems with an emphasis on the Japanese genres of haiku, senryu, tanka, and haibun. He was a recipient of the 2016 Touchstone Individual Poem Award for haiku, as granted by The Haiku Foundation. His work has been published in many journals (including Atlas Poetica, Presence, Modern Haiku and Acorn), and anthologies (including old song: The Red Moon Anthology of English-Language Haiku, 2017).

David He has been working as an advanced English teacher for 37 years in a high school. He has had more than twenty English-language short stories published in anthologies. His haiku have been published in *Acorn, The Heron's Nest, Presence, Rocket bottles, Frogpond, One Hundred Gourds, Shamrock, First Literary Review-East, Modern Haiku, Frozen Butterfly,* and elsewhere. He has also had tanka published in *Skylark, Ribbons, Red Lights Tanka of America* and *Cattails*

David Rice is the current editor of the Tanka Society of Ameria's triannual journal, *Ribbons*. He lives in Berkeley, California.

Debbie Strange (Canada) is a short form poet, photographer and haiga artist. She is the author of *Warp and Weft: Tanka Threads* (Keibooks 2015) and its sequel, *Three-Part Harmony: Tanka Verses*(Keibooks 2018). Please visit her at http://www.debbiemstrange.blogspot.ca.

Don Miller lives in the Chihuahuan Desert of southern New Mexico, USA. He has been writing tanka since the early 1980s, and has had his tanka, tanka sequences, tanka prose, and other short-form poetry published on a somewhat regular basis in various print and online journals since the early 2000s.

Don Wentworth is a Pittsburgh-based poet whose work reflects his interest in the revelatory nature of brief, haiku-like moments in everyday life. He is the author of three full-length collections: *Past All Traps* (2011), *Yield to the Willow* (2014) and *With a Deepening Presence* (2016). He is the long-time editor of the small press magazine, *Lilliput Review*.

Elizabeth Howard lives in Arlington, Tennessee. Her tanka have been published in *Eucalypt, red lights, Mariposa, Ribbons, Gusts, Atlas Poetica, Skylark, Moonbathing,* and other journals.

Geoffrey Winch is a retired highway engineer who lives close by England's south coast. He is associated with several creative writing groups and regularly reads his poetry at the Chichester Open Mic. His work has appeared in many small press journals and anthologies mainly in the UK, US and online, and he has published five collections, most recently *Alchemy of Vision* (Indigo Dreams, 2014) and *West Abutment Mirror Images* (O Original Plus, 2017).

Gerry Jacobson lives in a Canberra suburb. He has been writing tanka for ten years, enjoys the challenge of tanka sequences, and loves how it enables him to write about his experiences, memories, and feelings. He dotes on four grandchildren and visits them in Sydney and in Stockholm.

Giselle Maya is a painter and poet who lives in Provence, France. She has lived and studied in Japan. Presently she enjoys gardening, writing and, when time allows, painting. Some of her most recent publications are *The Tao of Water, Poem Tales, Garden Mandala, Anemones, Treewhispers, Shizuka* and *Cicada Chant.* Many well-known journals have published her work: *Ribbons, Skylark, Kokako, CHO, Haibun Today, Cattails, Editions des Petits Nuages* and several others. To order books please contact the author: giselle.maya@orange.fr.

Grunge is a gay Indo-American, who specializes in urban tanka. He currently lives in South Florida with a collection of pet arthropods, an ancient cat, and a pudgy leopard gecko.

Jan Foster, a former English teacher, lives with her husband in Geelong, Australia. Her tanka, tanka prose, haiku, haibun and responsive sequences have been published in journals in Japan, USA, New Zealand, Britain, Canada and Australia, as well as online. She is the founder of the Bottlebrush Tanka Group (Sydney) and the Breathstream Tanka Group (Geelong). Her favourite things, apart from writing with her responsive sequence partners, are her grandchildren, a good book to read, a cryptic crossword to conquer and a samurai Sudoku to solve.

Jayashree Maniyil lives in Melbourne, Australia. She started her journey of understanding and writing Japanese short forms of poetry (mainly haiku) in 2011. She continues to indulge in them on a casual basis. She was fortunate to have some of her verses published in reputed haiku journals in the past.

Jenny Ward Angyal lives with her husband and one Abyssinian cat on a small organic farm in Gibsonville, NC, USA. She has written poetry since the age of five and tanka since 2008. She is Reviews and Features Editor of *Skylark: A Tanka Journal.* Her tanka and other poems have appeared widely in print and online journals and may also be found on her tanka blog, The Grass Minstrel http://grassminstrel.blogspot.com/. Her tanka collection, *moonlight on water* (Skylark Publishing), appeared in 2016.

Jessica Malone Latham, M.A. is the author of *cricket song: Haiku and Short Poems from a Mother's Heart* (Red Moon Press) and chapbooks, *clouds of light* (wooden nickel press) and *all this bowing* (buddha baby press). Her poetry has appeared in dozens of journals and anthologies, and she is the recipient of several awards. Most recently, Jessica's poetry has been featured in the Seasons of Haiku path at Holden Arboretum in Ohio, and on Mann Library's Daily Haiku. To see more of Jessica's work, to purchase her collections, or consider taking one of her poetry courses, visit her website: www.jessicalatham.com.

Joanna Ashwell, a writer from the North East of England. Enjoys reading and writing tanka, haiku, Cherita and other related forms. Published in *Atlas Poetica, Eucalypt, Moonbathing, Skylark* and others. Enjoys peace, quiet, good wine and chocolate.

Josie Hibbing is a stay-home Mom of 8 kids. She enjoys writing haiku and tanka.

Joy McCall likes sequences although she writes a daily tanka as she has done for decades, her way of marking the days and places.

Julie Bloss Kelsey writes short-form poetry from her home in suburban Maryland. She enjoys travel, coffee, dogs, butterflies, and meeting new people. Connect with her on Twitter (@MamaJoules).

Kath Abela Wilson is a poet, artist and leader of Poets on Site. She hosts meetings in her home and at The Storrier Stearns Japanese Garden in Pasadena. She recently published Driftwood Monster (haiku) and An Owl Still Asking, (tanka) two short form chapbooks from Moria Press.

Larry Kimmel lives quietly in the hills of western Massachusetts. His most recent books are *shards and dust, outer edges* and *Side by Side* (with Joy McCall). *The Piercing Blue of Sirius: Selected Poems 1968–2008* is free to read online at: http://larrykimmel.tripod.com/the_piercing_blue_of_sirius.htm, Colrain, Massachusetts USA.

Laura Davis is a New Zealander who lives in Sydney, Australia, with her family. Laura is a member of the Fellowship of Australian Writers, the Tanka Huddle group, and writes tanka, haiku, prose and poetry for children.

Leslie Bamford is a published writer of short stories, poems and plays, and teacher of creative writing and memoir. She lives in Ontario, Canada. Since she retired, she fell in love with writing tanka, often composing while walking her dog and taking photographs. For more about her work, visit www.lesliebamford.com.

Lorne Henry lives in countryside New South Wales, Australia, but she has many memories of other parts of the world that sometimes surface. She has been writing haiku since 1992 and tanka from about 2005. She also writes haibun and tanka prose.

Luminita Suse is the author of the tanka collections *A Thousand Fireflies / Mille Lucioles* and *Winter Fire*, Editions des petits nuages, 2011 and 2016. Her poetry appeared in *Moonbathing: A Journal of Women's Tanka, Gusts, Atlas Poetica, Magnapoets, Red Lights, Ribbons, Take Five: Best Contemporary Tanka* 2010/2011, *Haiku Canada Review, Skylark*, and others. She received honourable mentions in The 7th and the 8th International Tanka Festival Competitions, 2012/2016, organized by Japan Tanka Poets' Society and Under the Basho, International Haiku Contest, 2014.

Lynne Leach emigrated from England to California but is still a Londoner at heart. A designer, gardener, and quilt artist, she finds poetry the sustaining element of her life. She and David Rice have been writing tanka together since 1996. Skylark Press published their book, *Lighting a Lamp: 20 Years of Tanka Conversations*, in 2017.

M. Kei is a tall ship sailor and award-winning poet who lives on Maryland's Eastern shore. He is the editor of *Stacking Stones, An Anthology of Short Tanka Sequences* and also *Atlas Poetica : A Journal of World Tanka*. His most recent collection of poetry is *January, A Tanka Diary*. He is also the author of the award-winning gay Age of Sail adventure novels, *Pirates of the Narrow Sea*s (blogspot.narrowseas.com). He can be followed on Twitter @kujakupoet, or visit AtlasPoetica.org.

Malintha Perera is an established poet whose work is featured in numerous journals. She writes haiku, tanka, micropoetry as well as longer poems that are mainly centered on Zen Buddhism. Her first published haiku book, *An Unswept Path* (2015) is a collection of monastery haiku. She resides in Sri Lanka with her family.

Marianne Paul is a poet, novelist, kayaker, and more recently, a bookbinder. She has won the Vancouver Cherry Blossom Festival haiku invitational contest (Canada division) and the Jane Reichhold Memorial Haiga Competition (mixed media category), and is a member of the Banyan Tree Poets.

Marilyn Humbert lives in the Northern suburbs of Sydney NSW Australia. Her tanka and haiku appear in international and Australian journals, anthologies and online. Some of her free verse poems have been awarded prizes in competitions and some have been published.

Marshall Bood lives in Regina, Saskatchewan, Canada. His poetry has recently *appeared in Presence, bottle rockets, Scryptic and Failed Haiku*.

Martin McKellar tends a Zen-style dry garden, collects vintage men's Japanese kimono and photographs people responding to contemplative spaces.

Mary Hohlman is published poet, Feng Shui consultant, and mama. She finds daily inspiration from the beautiful outdoors of Northern

California, her sweet daughter, and the many blessings of her life. www.maryhohlman.com.

Matsukaze is a classical opera singer in Texas, USA. He is a member of Tanka Society of America, a dedicated scholar of Japanese forms, and an experimentalist.

Matthew Caretti began composing short poems in 2009. His work has since appeared in numerous journals and anthologies, including *Take Five: Best Contemporary Tanka*, vol. 4, *Atlas Poetica: Geography and the Creative Imagination*, and *Atlas Poetica: Urban Tanka*. His poems have also garnered a few awards here and there. Matthew is now inspired daily by his work at Amitofo Care Centre, an orphanage of 278 children, in Ha Lumisi, Lesotho.

Michael G. Smith is a chemist. His poetry, tanka, haiku and haibun have been published in many literary journals and anthologies. *No Small Things* was published by Tres Chicas Books in 2014. *The Dippers Do Their Part*, a collaboration with visual artist Laura Young of haibun and katagami from their Shotpouch Cabin residency sponsored by the Spring Creek Project (Oregon State University), was published by Miriam's Well in 2015. His poem 'Disturbance Theory' was the first place winner of the Oregon Poetry Association's Fall 2017 Contest, New Poet category. He lives in the USA.

Originally from Detroit, Michigan, **Michael H. Lester** now lives in Los Angeles, California, where he practices business management and writes poetry. You can find his first book of poetry, *Notes from a Commode*, Volume I, on Amazon.com.

Mike Montreuil lives the retired life in Ottawa, Ontario. He is the editor of the *Haiku Canada Review* and co-editor of the French tanka journal *Cirrus: Tankas de nos jours*.

Miriam Sagan's haiku books are *Dream That Is Not A Dream*, with Elizabeth Searle Lamb, and *All My Beautiful Failures*. She participated in Axle Arts roadside haiku and renga in the Railyard projects. Sagan curated the installation of three metal signs on Santa Fe's westside which spell out a haiku by Chiyo-Ni. Her haiku have appeared on earrings, chairs, windows, ceramic sculpture, weathergrams, and in numerous publications internationally. She blogs at *Miriam's Well* (http://miriamswell.wordpress.com). She lives in the USA.

Neal Whitman lives in Pacific Grove, California with his wife, Elaine. The sights, sounds, and smells of Monterey Bay inspire his poetry and her photography. He is a docent at the Point Pinos Lighthouse in Pacific Grove which is the oldest, continuously operating lighthouse on the west coast of the United States. Neal is Vice President of the United Haiku and Tanka Society and was co-judge of the 2018 Tanka Society of America, Sanford Goldstein International Tanka Contest.

Patricia Prime grew up in England and now lives in New Zealand. Here she obtained a degree in English and Social Sciences and gained a Teaching Diploma. She taught kindergarten for 40 years. Patricia is the editor of *Kokako*, writes reviews for *Takahe, Atlas Poetica, Muse India* and other journals. She is reviews/interviews editor of *Haibun Today*. Her poetry, haiku, tanka, haibun, tanka prose and cherita have been published in a variety of journals and anthologies. Patricia published *Shizuka* with Giselle Maya

Peggy Castro write tanka, tanka sequences, haiku, haibun and tanka prose in Los Angeles CA, USA. She attends group meetings and writing sessions with Poets on Site in Pasadena and publishes in international journals.

Pravat Kumar Padhy, Scientist, and Poet, hails from Odisha, India. He holds Masters in Science and Technology and a Ph.D. from Indian Institute of Technology, Dhanbad. His Japanese short form of poetry appeared in various international journals and anthologies. His tanka are featured in anthologies *Fire Pearls 2, One Man's Maple Moon Bright Stars Vol. 1, Neon Graffiti, Triveni, Every Chicken, Cow, Fish and Frog: Animal Rights Haiku, Earth: Our Common Ground Anthology, They Gave Us Life* and others. His haiku won Vancouver Cherry Blossom Festival Honourable Mention Award, Canada, UNESCO International Year of Water Co-operation, The Kloštar Ivanić International Haiku Contest, Creatrix Haiku Commendation Award, IAFOR Vladimir Devide Haiku Award, 7th Setouchi Matsuyama International Photo Haiku Award and others.

Pris Campbell writes both free verse and short forms. Among other journals, her short forms have appeared in *cattails, Frogpond, Acorn, Hedgerow, Moonset* and *Failed Haiku*. Nixes Mate recently published her tanka book, *Squall Line on the Horizon*, which can be found on Amazon. A former Clinical Psychologist, sailer, and bicyclist, she was sidelined by ME/CFS in 1990 and leads a quieter life, devoted to her writing and graphics, in the Greater West Palm Beach, Florida.

Ram Krishna Singh, born, brought up and educated in Varanasi, India is a retired university professor, who has authored 42 books, including tanka and haiku collections such as *Sense and Silence: Collected Poems* (2010), *New and Selected Poems Tanka and Haiku* (2012), *I am No Jesus and Other Selected Poems, Tanka and Haiku* (2014), *God Too Awaits Light* (2017), and *Growing Within* (2017). He is widely anthologized in India and abroad and translated into many languages, including French,

Chinese, Japanese, Romanian, Italian, Crimean Tatar, Russian, German, Greek, Spanish, Farsi, Serbian, Croatian, Slovene, Bulgarian etc. Professor Singh has been associated with several journals and organizations. More at: http://rksinghpoet.blogspot.in.

Richard Grahn is an ever-aspiring poet/writer, sculptor, and photographer currently living in Chicago, Illinois USA. His poetic interests include various Japanese styles e.g. haiku, tanka, haibun and haiga. He also enjoys collaborative poetry across a variety of styles. He holds an Associate Degree in Fine Arts from Butte Community College in Oroville, California with additional studies at California State University, Chico.

Richard St. Clair (b. 1946) is both a poet and a composer of modern classical music. Born and raised in North Dakota, he came East to attend Harvard, from which he holds three degrees in music composition. As a pianist, he has recorded many of his works, some of which are on YouTube. His tanka have appeared in various Keibooks publications including *Bright Stars* and *Atlas Poetica*. He has lived in Massachusetts most of his adult life and is inspired by the natural beauty of New England.

Robert Bamford grew up in Kitchener, Ontario. He likes an adventure through boating, painting and hiking with his wife and dog. His passion for writing comes out in fiction, poetry (especially haiku and tanka), and memoir.

Robyn Cairns is a Melbourne based poet who loves writing short form poetry inspired by her local urban industrial surroundings and adventures in nature. She has been published widely in short form journals and has had two chapbooks published by Gininnderra Press. Robyn loves being a member of the Banyan Tree Poets who are very dear to her.

Roger Jones teaches at Texas State University in San Marcos. His haibun e-chapbook, *Goodbye*, was published in summer 2017.

Samar Ghose grew up in India, but lives in Australia with his wife and two daughters. Like many people who discover the Japanese short verse forms, he too enjoys reading them and occasionally attempts to write some.

Sanford Goldstein is now 92 years old. He has been writing tanka for more than fifty years. He continues to live in Japan with his friend Kazuaki Wakui.

Susan Burch is a good egg.

Tamara K. Walker resides in Colorado and writes short fiction, often of a surreal, irreal, magical realist, experimental or otherwise unusual flavor, and poetry, often in originally East Asian forms adapted into English. Her tanka have appeared or are forthcoming in *Ribbons, Eucalypt, Moonbathing : a journal of women's tanka, Atlas Poetica: A Journal of World Tanka, LYNX, A Hundred Gourds, Star*Line* and *Scifaikuest*. Her poetry in other forms has been published in *Lavender Review, Eastern Structures, The Ghazal Page,* and *the cherita,* as well as other places.

Taura Scott reads and writes tanka at her home in sunny Southern California. Her work can be found in *Atlas Poetica, Ribbons, red lights, Skylark* and other publications. She is a long time member of Poets on Site and the Caltech Red Door poets.

Tiffany Shaw-Diaz is an award-winning poet who has been featured in *Modern Haiku, Frogpond, Acorn, Presence,* and dozens of other publications. She is the founder and director of The Co-op Poetry Lab.

Tish Davis lives in northern Ohio. Her work has appeared in various journals including *Modern Haiku, tinywords, Frogpond, Atlas Poetica, Skylark, Haibun Today, Ribbons, Contemporary Haibun Online* and others. When she isn't busy with work and grandchildren, she enjoys exploring the local parks with her husband and three dogs.

Tracy Davidson lives in Warwickshire, England, and writes poetry and flash fiction. Her work has appeared in various publications and anthologies, including: *Poet's Market, Mslexia, Atlas Poetica, Writing Magazine, Modern Haiku, The Binnacle, A Hundred Gourds, Shooter, Journey to Crone, The Great Gatsby Anthology, WAR* and *In Protest: 150 Poems for Human Rights.*

Vasile Moldovan is a Romanian poet, especially of haiku. But he published tanka too in *Atlas Poetica* (USA), *Albatros, Haiku* (Romania) and I other magazines. He signs several haiku books and one of tanka, bilingual, English/Romanian, *After the Tempest / După furtună* (Bucharest, România, 2013).

Vijay Joshi is a published poet, having published *Reflective Musings,* a collection of contemporary poems and *Kaleidoscope of poems,* a collection of haibun, tanka poems. His poems are published in *Haibun Today, Chrysanthemum, and Contemporary Haibun,* and *Atlas Poetica.*

Index

Publications by Keibooks

Anthologies

Neon Graffiti : Tanka of Urban Life

Bright Stars, An Organic Tanka Anthology (Vols. 1 – 7)

Take Five : Best Contemporary Tanka (Vol. 4)

Fire Pearls (Vols. 1 – 2) : Short Masterpieces of the Heart

Tanka Collections

Three-Part Harmony, by Debbie Strange NEW!

Warp and Weft, Tanka Threads, by Debbie Strange

Black Genji and Other Contemporary Tanka, by Matsukaze

October Blues and Other Contemporary Tanka, by Matsukaze

flowers to the torch : American Tanka Prose, by peter fiore

on the cusp encore, a year of tanka, by Joy McCall
fieldgates, tanka sequences, by Joy McCall
on the cusp, a year of tanka, by Joy McCall
rising mist, fieldstones, by Joy McCall
hedgerows, tanka pentaptychs, by Joy McCall
*circling smoke, scattered bone*s, by Joy McCall

Tanka Left Behind 1968 : Tanka from the Notebooks of Sanford Goldstein, by Sanford Goldstein
Tanka Left Behind : Tanka from the Notebooks of Sanford Goldstein, by Sanford Goldstein
This Short Life, Minimalist Tanka, by Sanford Goldstein

Journals

Atlas Poetica : A Journal of World Tanka

M. Kei's Poetry Collections

January, A Tanka Diary

Slow Motion : The Log of a Chesapeake Bay Skipjack
tanka and short forms

Heron Sea : Short Poems of the Chesapeake Bay
tanka and short forms

M. Kei's Novels

Pirates of the Narrow Seas 1 : The Sallee Rovers
Pirates of the Narrow Seas 2 : Men of Honor
Pirates of the Narrow Seas 3 : Iron Men
Pirates of the Narrow Seas 4 : Heart of Oak

Man in the Crescent Moon : A Pirates of the Narrow Seas Adventure
The Sea Leopard : A Pirates of the Narrow Seas Adventure

Fire Dragon

Made in the
USA
Monee, IL